The Sacred Pipe

Frank Fools Crow praying with the Sacred Pipe at the dedication of St. Isaac Jogues Church in Rapid City, S.D. With permission of the Diocese of Rapid City Archives.

The Sacred Pipe

An Archetypal Theology

Paul B. Steinmetz, S.J.

Syracuse University Press

First Edition 1998
98 99 00 01 02 03   6 5 4 3 2 1

Chapter 5, "The Ethnology of the Sacred Pipe," first published as a special issue of the *American Indian Culture and Research Journal* 8, no. 3 (1986): 27– 80, is published here in a slightly revised form. Permission to reprint that article is gratefully acknowledged.

The paper used in this publication meets the minimum requirements of American National Standard for Information Sciences — Permanence of Paper for Printed Library Materials, ANSI Z39.48-1984. ∞™

Library of Congress Cataloging-in-Publication Data
Steinmetz, Paul B.
The sacred pipe : an archetypal theology / Paul B. Steinmetz. —
1st ed.
p.   cm.
Includes bibliographical references and index.
ISBN 0-8156-0544-7 (cloth : alk. paper)
1. Oglala Indians — Rites and ceremonies.   2. Oglala Indians —
Religion.   3. Oglala mythology.   4. Calumets — Religious aspects.
5. Catholic Church — Missions — United States — History.
6. Christianity and culture — United States.   7. Popular culture —
Religious aspects — Catholic Church.   I. Title.
E99.O8S74   1998
299'.74 — dc21   98-24294

To Dr. Åke Hultkrantz,

an international authority whose research will remain
a major influence on the study of Native American religions
for many years to come, for being a mentor who recognized
my contribution to Oglala Lakota religion
and to him and his wife, Gerry, for their warm friendship

Paul B. Steinmetz, S.J. is a Jesuit priest who worked among the Oglala Lakota on the Pine Ridge Reservation in South Dakota for twenty years from 1961 to 1981. Father Steinmetz is the author of *Meditations with Native Americans: Lakota Spirituality* and *Pipe, Bible, and Peyote Among the Oglala Lakota: A Study in Religious Identity* reprinted by Syracuse University Press. As a visiting professor he taught Native American religions at the University of California in Los Angeles and at Marquette University in Milwaukee. He is presently an associate pastor at the Church of Santa Maria in Orinda, California.

Contents

The Sacred Pipe

Prologue

On November 6, 1965, a beautiful fall day, in a cemetery
on the top of a hill in the Slim Butte Community on the
Pine Ridge Reservation in South Dakota I stood praying
with the Sacred Pipe at the funeral of Rex Long Visitor. I
held up a pipe filled with tobacco, and taking the stem
and bowl apart, I said: "Remember man, that the pipe of
your life some day will be broken." I then laid the separated pipe on the coffin. After the prayers from the Catholic ritual, I took up the two separated pieces and putting
them together I said, "Through the resurrection of Christ
the life of Rex Long Visitor and all of us will be brought
together into eternal happiness." Then I paraphrased
Scripture, repeating in the four directions: "I am the Living and Eternal Pipe, the Resurrection and the Life; whoever believes in Me and dies shall live, and whoever
believes in Me shall never suffer eternal death." After the
fourth direction, I touched the bowl of the pipe to the
earth in silence.

The Lakota people crowded around the grave were

filled with both bewilderment and admiration, and they immediately asked John Iron Rope, the medicine man of that community who was present at the ceremony, whether the prayer I offered with the Sacred Pipe was proper. He assured them that it was, indeed, proper. Here was a Lakota medicine man affirming the Sacred Pipe as an image of Christ. One Lakota complained, however, that a pipe filled with tobacco should never be taken apart because it is against the customary way of handling the pipe. He missed the whole point of the symbolism because that is the very reason a separated pipe is an image of death.

My intuition was confirmed in a Vision Quest that I made under the direction of the medicine man Pete Catches. I fasted for two days and two nights on a hill on the ground made sacred by the string of tobacco pouches around the four colored flags. I fasted with the pipe filled with tobacco in my hands and the pyx with the conse-crated host, the Body of Christ, around my neck, follow-ing a request that Catches made to me. My vision was an overwhelming sense of the cosmic presence of Christ in the world of creation and of the sacramental presence of Christ in the Eucharistic host, two real, but different, presences. In that Vision Quest I was called to discover that Christ was indeed present in the Sacred Pipe and in the consecrated host as well.

My intuition would also be confirmed from another source. Ten years later, while researching the Sacred Pipe for a master's degree at the University of Aberdeen in Scotland, I read Clark Wissler's *Societies and Ceremonial*

Associations in the Oglala Division of the Teton Dakota. I discovered that in every war party there was a pipe man who carried no weapons and did no fighting. His purpose was to pray. Before going out on the warpath, he took apart a filled pipe, leaving the filled bowl in the camp and taking the stem with him. If they returned victorious, he put the pieces together and prayed in celebration. If they were killed, the separated pieces became a symbol of death (1912, 15). I had the same intuition as a Lakota medicine man very likely had had several hundred years before. The same unconscious bridged the centuries and brought us close together.*

I still was not satisfied. I wanted a more mature understanding. The intuition did come from my unconscious, but how and why was it activated? The search for the answer to this question led me to develop an archetypal theology of the Sacred Pipe as an image of Christ.

I draw from the ethnology of the Sacred Pipe as David Miller did from Greek mythology in his *Christs: Meditation on Archetypal Images in Christian Theology.*

> But the locating of the images in the theological ideas is not only a historical and Biblical task. The perspective here is rather to view such images as *archetypal.* By this is meant just what the word originally implied. *Typos* denoted the imprint made by a sculpted ring when it

---

* Symbols, however, are multivalent. The medicine man also believed that the stem would bring the war party back to the bowl. But this does not invalidate the above intuition because it is most likely that he also recognized the symbol of death in the separated pieces.

was pressed on warm wax. It has to do with the forms of pressure and suggests noting where a person is impressed or de-pressed. It has to do with what strikes one. To add the prefix, *arche*, deepens the idea. It is not just any striking or impression, but rather the most fundamental, archaic, deepest, most original one. Thus, viewed as *archetypal theology*, which is one way to think of this project, there is an attempt to deal with the images within theological ideas where they press on the life of the self or *psyche* ("soul") most profoundly. (1981, xx)

Miller argues that Christian theologians to articulate the faith borrowed Greek philosophical thought-forms which, in turn, were borrowed from the poets and myth-makers. "This means that philosophical concepts were just another vocabulary, now formal and logical, for the mythopoetic stories of the gods told by Homer and Hesiod" (xviii). Consequently "behind the doctrine of Christ who is thought of in the image of the Good Shepherd, there is not only Pan, the god of 'pastoral' care, but also Polyphemos, the one-eyed monster. Behind Christ the Great Teacher is not only Socrates, but also Silenos lying drunk in a deep cave of myth" (xx).

My argument is that because Christian images are derived from a common religious substratum expressed through primal religions, behind the image of Christ is the image of the Sacred Pipe and its many associations. Although the ethnology of the Sacred Pipe is the primary source of these images, my past experience of Lakota reli-

gion on the Pine Ridge Reservation and the challenges of
ministry there for twenty years are included insofar as
they contribute to this development.

A personal journey through the thoughts of Mircea
Eliade, Carl Jung, and Karl Rahner helped lead me to
discover this more mature understanding of the intuition
of the Sacred Pipe as an archetypal image of Christ that I
had on the top of the hill. It also enabled me to develop a
model of religious identity that served as a psychological
foundation. The reader is invited to make the same journey. Although this journey may take some time and perse-
verance because the reader may have to reread and
meditate on some of the material, reading this book will
certainly facilitate the journey because it contains those
texts and insights that are most essential for reaching the
destination. A journey of some thirty years cannot be
taken in a single day.

In the first chapter I share the contributions made by
the phenomenology of Mircea Eliade, in the second those
of the depth psychology of Carl Jung, and in the third
those of the theology of Karl Rahner. I use rather extensive quotations from these authors derived from several
thousand pages of text so that the reader can share in
the same journey I made. This part of the book can be
considered a mini reader of these three authors, which
saves the reader from the need to consult twenty-two separate volumes. The reading of this material is essential for
understanding chapter 4. There I arrive at some original
insights method by making intuitive identifications. In
doing this I discovered that no single discipline can give a

total understanding of reality, but disciplines need each other. In chapter 5 I present the source of these images in a comprehensive ethnology of the Sacred Pipe among Native Americans. In chapter 6 I develop the archetype of the Sacred Pipe and its many associations as images of Christ. Then, I share my vision at the end of the journey in an epilogue, present scholarly evaluations of Eliade, Jung, and Rahner in an appendix, and provide an extensive bibliography, which gives the reader access to the most important literature for further exploration.

1

The Phenomenology of Mircea Eliade

As a newly ordained Jesuit priest, I read Mircea Eliade's Patterns in Comparative Religion, *which had a profound influence on my life. He gave me a whole new understanding of so-called "pagan idolatry" that was not contained in the Bible. St. Paul repeated what the Old Testament prophets had said throughout the centuries: "While claiming to be wise, they became fools and exchanged the glory of the immortal God for the likeness of an image of mortal man or of birds or of four legged animals or of snakes. . . . They exchanged the truth of God for a lie and revered and worshiped the creature rather then the creator" (Rom. 1:22–23, 25 NAB). Eliade, however, presented an entirely different interpretation of "pagan idolatry," one in which the non-Christian did not worship the creature. It became evident to me that Paul was not presenting an objective view of "pagan idolatry" but addressing early Christians to keep them from relapsing into the practices of primal religions. In Eliade's words:*

In the so-called "worship of stones" not all stones are held to be sacred. We shall always find that some stones are venerated because they are a certain shape, or because they are very large, or because they are bound up with some ritual. Note, too, that it is not a question of actually worshiping the stones — the stones are venerated precisely because they are not simply stones but hierophanies, something outside their normal status as things. The dialectic of a hierophany implies a more or less clear choice, a singling-out. A thing becomes sacred insofar as it embodies (that is, reveals) something other than itself (Eliade 1958, 13).

But Eliade would go even farther than this in giving "pagan idolatry" a Christo-centric meaning.

One could attempt to vindicate the hierophanies which preceded the miracle of the Incarnation in the light of Christian teaching, by showing their importance as a series of prefigurations of that Incarnation. Consequently, far from thinking of pagan religious ways (fetishes, idols and such) as false and degenerate stages in the religious feeling of mankind fallen in sin, one may see them as desperate attempts to prefigure the mystery of the Incarnation. The whole religious life of mankind — expressed in the dialectic of hierophanies — would, from this standpoint, be simply a waiting for Christ (Eliade 1958, 30n).

So Eliade proposed a continuity between primal religions and Christianity.

Here, at the conclusion of this, I should like simply to declare that almost all the religious attitudes man has, he has had from the most primitive times. From one point of view there has been no break in continuity from the "primitives "to Christianity. The dialectic of the hierophany remains one, whether in an Australian *churinga* or in the Incarnation of the Logos. In both cases we are faced with a manifestation, vastly different obviously, of the sacred in a fragment of the universe (Eliade 1958, 463).

Eliade also gave me a vision of the cosmic presence of Christ in creation.

Some of the highest religious experiences identify the sacred with the whole universe. To many a mystic the integrated quality of the cosmos is itself a hierophany. "The whole universe, from Brahma down to a blade of grass is one form or another of Him" exclaims the *Mahanirvana Tantra*, taking up an extremely old and well-known Indian saying. This "He", *Atman-Brahman*, is manifest everywhere. . . . That this is more than a simple idea classed, rightly or wrongly, as pantheist, is shown by the words of Leon Bloy speaking of the "mystery of Life, which is Christ: *Ego sum Vita*. Whether the Life is in men, animals or plants, it is always Life, and when the moment, the imperceptible instant called death comes, it is always Christ who withdraws, as much from a tree as from a human being" (Eliade 1958, 459).

I learned about the nature of symbolism. First, archetypal images cannot be taken literally but have multivalent meanings.

Philosophically, these problems of the "origin" and of the "true interpretation" of the Images are pointless. We need only remember that the attraction to the mother, if we interpret it on the plane of the immediate and "concrete" — like the desire to possess one's own mother — can *never tell us anything more than what it says;* whereas, if we take account of the fact that what is in question is the Image of the Mother, this desire means many things at once, for it is the desire to re-enter into the bliss of living Matter that is still "unformed", with all its possible lines of development, cosmological, anthropological, etc. . . . Images by their very structure are *multivalent.* If the mind makes use of images to grasp the ultimate reality of things, it is just because reality manifests itself in contradictory ways and therefore cannot be expressed in concepts (Eliade 1991, 15).

Phenomenology confirms the power of archetypal symbols.

In short, the majority of men "without religion" still hold to pseudo religions and degenerated mythologies. There is nothing surprising in this, for, as we saw, profane man is the descendant of *homo religiosus* and he cannot wipe out his own history — that is, the behavior of his religious ancestors which has made him what he is today. This is all the more true because a great part of his existence is fed by impulses that come to him from the depths of his being, from the zone that has been called the "un-conscious." A purely rational man is an abstraction; he is never found in real life. Every human being is made up at once of his conscious activity and his irrational experiences. Now, the contents and structures of the unconscious exhibit astonishing similarities to mythological images and figures. We do not mean to say that mythologies are the "product" of the unconscious, for the mode of being of the myth is precisely that *it reveals itself as myth*, that is, it announces that something *has been manifested in a paradigmatic manner*(Eliade 1961, 209–10).

Because the unconscious is the result of countless existential experiences, it must resemble the religious experiences outside the psyche that activated the archetypes.

Yet the contents and structures of the unconscious are the result of immemorial existential situations, especially of critical situations, and this is why the unconscious has a religious aura. For every existential crisis once again puts in question both the reality of the world and man's presence in the world. This means that the existential crisis is, finally, "religious," since on the archaic levels of culture *being* and the *sacred* are one. As we saw, it is the experience of the sacred that founds the world, and even the most elementary religion is, above all, an ontology. In other words, insofar as the unconscious is the result of countless existential experiences, it cannot but resemble the various religious universes (Eliade 1961, 210).

Symbols open humans to transcendent reality, to the world of the spirit.

For religion is the paradigmatic solution for every existential crisis. It is the paradigmatic solution not only because it can be indefinitely repeated, but also because it is believed to have a transcendental origin and hence is valorized as a revelation received from an *other*, transhuman world. The religious solution not only resolves the crisis but at the same time makes existence "open" to values that are no longer contingent or particular, thus enabling man to transcend personal situations and, finally, gain access to the world of spirit (Eliade 1961, 210).

It follows that he who understands a symbol not only "opens out" to the objective world, but at the same time succeeds in emerging from his particular situation and in attaining a comprehension of the universal. This is explained by the fact that symbols have a way of causing immediate reality, as well as particular situations, to "burst." Whenever a tree incarnates the World Tree or when a spade is associated with the phallus and agricultural work with the act of generation, for example, one could say that the immediate reality of these objects or actions "bursts" or "explodes" under the irruptive force of a more profound reality. The same might be said of an individual situation, let us say, that of the neophyte locked up in the initiation hut. The symbolism "bursts" the bonds of this particular situation, making it exemplary, that is to say, indefinitely repeatable in many and varied contexts (because the initiation hut is likened to the maternal womb and at the same time to the belly of a monster and to Hell, and the darkness symbolizes the Cosmic Night, the preformal, the fetal state of the world, etc.). Consequently, because of the symbol, the individual experience is "awakened" and transmuted in a spiritual act. To "live" a symbol and to decipher its message correctly implies an opening toward the Spirit and, finally, access to the universal (Eliade 1959, 103).

This openness to the spirit is the symbol's purpose.

The unconscious activity of modern man ceaselessly presents him with innumerable symbols, and each of them has a particular message to transmit, a particular mission to accomplish, in order to ensure or to re-establish the equilibrium of the psyche. As we have seen, the symbol not only makes the world "open" but also helps religious man to attain to the universal. For it is through symbols that man finds his way out of his particular situation and "opens himself" to the general and the universal. Symbols awaken individual experience and transmute it into a spiritual act, into metaphysical comprehension of the world. In the presence of any tree, symbol of the world tree and image of cosmic life, a man of the premodern societies can attain to the highest spirituality, for, by understanding the symbol, *he succeeds in living the universal.* The image of the tree still quite frequently appears in the imaginary universes of modern nonreligious man; it is a cipher of his deeper life, of the drama that is played out in his unconscious and that concerns the integrity of his psychomental

life and hence his own existence. But as long as the symbol
of the tree does not awaken his total consciousness and
"open" it to the universe, it cannot be said to have completely fulfilled its function. It has only partly "saved" him
from his individual situation — for example, by enabling
him to resolve a deep crisis and restoring his temporarily
threatened psychic equilibrium; but it has not yet raised
him to spirituality — that is, it has not succeeded in revealing one of the structures of the real to him (Eliade 1961,
211–12).

*Failure to recognize the symbol's purpose is in Christian terms a
new "fall."*

This example, it seems to us, suffices to show in what
way the nonreligious man of modern societies is still nour-
ished and aided by the activity of his unconscious yet
without thereby attaining to a properly religious experience and vision of the world. The unconscious offers him
solutions for the difficulties of his own life, and in this way
plays the role of religion, for, before making an existence
a creator of values, religion ensures its integrity. From one
point of view it could almost be said that in the case of
those moderns who proclaim that they are nonreligious,
religion and mythology are "eclipsed" in the darkness of
their unconscious — which means too that in such men the
possibility of reintegrating a religious vision of life lies at
a great depth. Or, from the Christian point of view, it
could also be said that nonreligion is equivalent to a new
"fall" of man in other words, that nonreligious man has

lost the capacity to live religion consciously, and hence to understand and assume it; but that, in his deepest being, he still retains a memory of it, as, after the first "fall," his ancestor, the primordial man, retained intelligence enough to enable him to rediscover the traces of God that are visible in the world. After the first "fall," the religious sense descended to the level of the "divided" consciousness; now, after the second, it has fallen even further, into the depths of the unconscious; it has been "forgotten" (Eliade 1961, 212–13).

Transconscious experiences are amplifications of the archetypes in the unconscious.

Here, let us be content with the conclusion that we have to do with nonhistorical expressions of the same archetypal symbolism, manifesting itself in a coherent and systematic manner on the plane of the "unconscious" (of dream, hallucination or waking dream) as well as upon those of the "trans-conscious" and the conscious (aesthetic vision, ritual, mythology . . .) And let us emphasise, by the way, that the manifestations of the unconscious and the subconscious present values, and a structure, that are in perfect agreement with those of the conscious manifestations. . . .

Provisionally, then, let us accept the hypothesis that at least a certain zone of the subconscious is ruled by the archetypes which also dominate and organise conscious and transconscious experience. Hence we are entitled to regard the multiple variants of the same complexes of

symbols (such as those of "ascension" and of "binding")
as endless successions of "forms" which, on the different
levels of dream, myth, ritual, theology, mysticism, meta-
physics, etc., are trying to "realise" the archetype (Eliade
1991, 119–20).

*Most of all, Eliade taught me that symbols were necessary for
understanding the mystery of Christ. For example, the Christian
symbol of baptism gives new meaning to aquatic symbolism without destroying its primal values.*

In our retracing of the main outlines of the aquatic
symbology, [as a reservoir of all the potentialities of existence and immersion in as a reintegration into the undif-
ferentiated mode of preexistence in order to be
regenerated] we kept one precise point in view — namely,
the new religious values conferred upon Water by Christianity. The Fathers of the Church did not fail to exploit
some of the pre-Christian and universal values of the
Water-symbolism, retaining freedom to enrich it with new
meanings in relation to the Christian historical drama (Eliade 1991, 153).

As we see, the interpretations given by Tertullian [the
Holy Spirit hovering over the water] and John Chrysos-
tom [entombment and resurrection] harmonise perfectly
with the structure of aquatic symbol. However, certain
new elements that enter into this Christian revaluation of
Water are bound up with a "history"namely, Sacred History (154). Careful above all to attach themselves to a
history which is at the same time a *revelation*, careful not to

be confused with the "initiates" of the various religions and mysteries, the multiple gnosticisms that were swarming around the dying world of antiquity, the Fathers of the Church were obliged to take up the polemical position that they did. To reject all "paganism" was indispensable for the triumph of the message of the Christ. We may wonder whether this polemical attitude is still as strictly necessary in our own day (Eliade 1991, 157). . . .

It seems evident that the Judeo-Christian symbolism of baptism in no way contradicts the universally diffused symbolism of water. Everything reappears in it: Noah and the Flood have their counterparts in numerous traditions where some cataclysm puts an end to a whole "humanity" (or "society") with the exception of a single man who becomes the mythical Ancestor of a new humanity. The "Waters of Death" are the *leitmotif* of various palaeo-oriental, Asiatic, and Oceanian mythologies. The "Water" is pre-eminently "killing": it dissolves, it abolishes all forms. That is just why it is rich in creative "seeds". . . . The monsters of the abyss reappear in a number of traditions: the Heroes, the Initiates, go down into the depths of the abyss to confront marine monsters; this is a typical ordeal of initiation. Variants indeed abound: sometimes a dragon mounts guard over a "treasure" — a sensible image of the sacred, of absolute reality. The ritual (that is, initiatory) victory over the monstrous guardian is equivalent to the conquest of immortality. For the Christian, baptism is a sacrament because it was instituted by the Christ. But, none the less for that, it repeats the initiatory ritual of the ordeal (i.e., the struggle against the monster), of death and of the symbolic resurrection (the birth of the new man). I am not saying that Judaism or Christianity have "borrowed" such myths or such symbols from the religions of neighboring peoples — that was not necessary. Judaism had inherited a long religious history and prehistory in which all these things existed already. It was not even necessary that this or that symbol should have been kept "awake" in its integrity by Judaism; it was enough that a group of images survived, though obscurely, from pre-Mosaic times: such images were capable of conveying, at no matter what moment, a powerful religious actuality (Eliade 1991, 158–59).

Christian revelation does not destroy the primary meaning of archetypal images.

Certain Fathers of the Church have examined the interesting correspondence between the archetypal images evoked by Christianity and the images which are the common property of mankind. One of their most constant concerns is, precisely, to make manifest to unbelievers the correspondence between those great symbols which the soul finds immediately expressive and persuasive, and the dogmas of the new religion. Speaking to those who deny the resurrection of the dead, Theophilus of Antioch appeals to the signs that God puts within their reach in those great phenomena of Nature, the beginning and end of the seasons, and of day and night. He goes so far as to say: "Is there not a resurrection for the seeds and the fruits?" For Clement of Rome, "day and night show us the resurrection: the night descends, the day breaks; the day departs and night arrives" (Beirnaert 1949, 275; 1951, 79). For the Christian apologists, the Images were charged with signs and messages; they showed forth the sacred by means of the cosmic rhythms. The revelation conveyed by the Faith did not dispel the "primary" meanings of the images; it simply added a new value to them. For the believer, it is true, this new meaning eclipsed all others: it alone valorised the image, transfiguring it into Revelation. It was the Resurrection of the Christ that mattered, and not the "signs" that one could read in Nature: in the majority of cases, one did not understand the "signs" until after having found the Faith in the depths of one's soul. But the mystery of faith is a matter for Christian experience, for theology and religious psychology and surpasses our present research. In the perspective I have chosen, one thing alone is important: that *every new valorisation has always been conditioned by the actual structure of the Image,* so much so that we can say of an Image that it is *awaiting* the fulfillment of its meaning (Eliade 1991, 159–60).

Proceeding to an analysis of the baptismal Images, the Rev. Fr. Beirnaert recognises "a relation between the dogmatic statements, the symbology of the Christian religion and the archetypes activated by the natural symbols. How, moreover, could the candidates for baptism understand the symbolic images put before them if these did not respond to their obscure expectations?" (Beirnaert 1949, 276; 1951, 79) The author is not surprised that "many Catholics should have rediscovered the way of faith through such experiences" (Beirnaert 1949, 276, 1951,

79–80). Of course, continues Fr. Beirnaert, the experience of the archetypes does not encroach upon the experience of the faith: "People may meet together in a common recognition of the relations of religious symbols to the psyche, and still class themselves as believers or as unbelievers" (Beirnaert 1949, 276–88; 1951, 79–80) . . . .Fr. Beirnaert recognises that, even if the imagery and symbolism of the Christian sacraments do not direct the believer's mind "primarily to the myths and immanent archetypes, but to the intervention of the divine Power in history, still new meaning must not lead us to deny the permanence of the ancient meaning. By its renewal of the great figures and symbolisations of natural religion, Christianity has also renewed their vitality and their power in the depths of the psyche. The mythic and archetypal dimension remains none the less real for being henceforth subordinate to another. The Christian may well be a man who has ceased to look for his spiritual salvation in myths and in experience of the immanent archetypes alone; he has not, for all that, abandoned all that the myths and symbolisms mean and do to the psychic man, to the microcosm. The adoption, by Christ and the Church, of the great images of the sun, the moon, of wood, water, the sea and so forth, amounts to in evangelisation of the effective powers that they denote. The Incarnation must not be reduced to the taking-on of the flesh alone. God has intervened even in the collective unconscious, that it may be saved and fulfilled. The Christ descended into hell. How, then, can this salvation reach into our unconsciousness without speaking its language and making use of its categories?"

(Beirnaert 1949, 284–85; 1951, 83–84) (Eliade 1991, 160–61). This text provides some important elucidations of the relations between "immanent symbols" and faith. As we have seen, the problem of faith lies outside our present deliberations. One aspect of it, however, is of interest to us: the Christian faith is dependent on a *historic* revelation: it is the manifestation of God in time which, in the eyes of a Christian, ensures the validity of the Images and the symbols. We have seen that the "immanent" and universal symbology of water was not abolished nor dismembered in consequence of the local and historical Judeo-Christian interpretations of baptismal symbolism. To put it in a rather simplified way: history does not radically modify the structure of an "immanent" symbolism. History continually adds new meanings to it, but these do not destroy the structure of the symbol (Eliade 1991, 161).

The structure of an archetypal symbol can only be discovered in the similarities of diverse historical manifestations.

Are we in fact condemned to be content with exhaustive analyses of "particular versions" which, when all is said and done, represent local histories? Have we no means of approach to the Image, the symbol, the archetype, in their own structures; in that "wholeness" which embraces all their "histories", without, however, confusing them? There are numerous patristic and liturgical texts which compare the Cross to a ladder, a column or a mountain. . . . And these, we may remember, are universally attested formulas for the "Centre of the World". It is in this aspect, as a symbol of the Centre of the World, that the Cross has been likened to the Cosmic Tree; which is a proof that the Image of the Centre *imposed itself naturally* upon the Christian mind. It is by the Cross (= the Centre) that communication with Heaven is opened and that, by the same token, the entire Universe is "saved". But *the notion of "salvation" does no more than repeat and complete the notions of perpetual renovation and cosmic regeneration, of universal fecundity and of sanctity, of absolute reality and, in the final reckoning, of immortality* — all of which co-exist in the symbolism of the Tree of the World.

Let it be well understood that I am not denying the importance of history, or in the case of Judeo-Christianity of faith, for the estimation of the true value of this or that symbol *as it was understood and lived in a specific culture:* we shall indeed underline this later. But it is not by "placing" a symbol in its own history that we can resolve the essential problem — namely, to know what is revealed to us, not by any "particular version" of a symbol but by the whole of a symbolism. We have already seen how the various meanings of a symbol are linked together, inter-connected in a system, as it were. The contradictions one can discover between the various particular versions are in most cases only apparent; they are resolved as soon as we consider the symbolism as a whole and discern its structure. Each new valorisation of an archetypal Image crowns and consummates the earlier ones: the "salvation" revealed by the Cross does not annul the pre-Christian values of the Tree of the World, that pre-eminent symbol of the total *renovatio;* on the contrary, the Cross comes to complete all its earlier valencies and meanings." Let us observe, once more, that this new valorisation, brought about by the identification of the Cosmic Tree with the Cross, took place in history and through a historical event—the Passion of Christ. As we shall see, the great originality of Judeo-Christianity was the transfiguration of History into theophany (Eliade 1991, 163–64).

Christian history and primal mythology have the same archetypal source, making particular history universal.

Note, here again, that the "intervention of God in history," that is, the divine revelation vouchsafed in Time renews and confirms a "non-temporal situation". The revelation that Judeo-Christianity alone received in a historical time which is never repeated, and which issues in the making of an irreversible history, was already preserved by archaic humanity in mythic form; nevertheless, the mystical experience of the "primitives" as well as the mystical life of Christians expresses itself through this same archetype—the re-entry into the original Paradise. We can clearly see that history—in this case, Sacred History —has brought no innovation. Among the primitives as among Christians, it is always a paradoxical return *in illud tempus,* a "leap backwards" abolishing time and history, that constitutes the mystical re-entry into Paradise. Consequently, although Biblical and Christian symbolism is charged with a historical and in the last analysis "provincial" content (since every local history is provincial in relation to universal history conceived in its totality), it remains nevertheless universal, like every coherent symbolism. We may even wonder whether the accessibility of Christianity may not be attributable in great measure to its symbolism, whether the universal Images that it takes up in its turn have not considerably facilitated the diffusion of its message. For, to the non-Christian, one question occurs first of all: how can a local history—that of the Jewish people and of the first Judeo-Christian communities—how can this claim to have become the pattern for all divine manifestation in concrete historical Time? I believe we have pointed to the answer: this sacred history, although in the eyes of an alien observer it looks like a local history, is also an exemplary history, because it takes up and perfects these trans-temporal Images (Eliade 1991, 168–69).

The primal religions of Europe rediscovered their own archetypes through Christianity.

The Images provide "openings" into a trans-historical world. That is by no means their least value: thanks to them, the different "histories" can intercommunicate. Much has been said about the unification of Europe by Christianity: and it is never better attested than when we see how Christianity coordinated the popular religious traditions. It was by means of Christian hagiography that the local cults—from Thrace to Scandinavia and from the Tagus to the Dnieper—were brought under a "common denominator." By the fact of their Christianisation, the gods and the sacred places of the whole of Europe not only received common names but rediscovered, in a sense, their own archetypes and therefore their universal valencies: a fountain in Gaul, regarded as sacred ever since prehistoric times, but sanctified by the presence of a divine local or regional figure, became sacred *for Christianity as a whole* after its consecration to the Virgin Mary. All the slayers of dragons were assimilated to Saint George or to some other Christian hero; all the Gods of the storm to holy Elijah. From having been regional and provincial, the popular mythology became ecumenical. It is, above all, through the creation of a new mythological language common to all the populations who remained attached to their soil — and therefore in the greater danger of becoming insulated in their own ancestral traditions — that the civilising mission of Christianity has been so remarkable. For, by Christianising the ancient European religious heritage, it not only purified the latter, but took up, into the new spiritual dispensation of mankind, all that deserved to be "saved" of the old practices, beliefs and hopes of pre-Christian man. Even today, in popular Christianity, there are rites and beliefs surviving from the neolithic: the boiled grain in honour of the dead, for instance (the *coliva* of Eastern and Agean Europe). The Christianisation of the peasant levels of Europe was effected thanks above all to the images: everywhere they were rediscovered, and had only to be revalorised, reintegrated and given new names (Eliade 1991, 174–75).

A meaning of a symbol in its maturity may have been vaguely grasped in earlier times.

All this could be formulated in another manner. Symbols are capable of being understood on more and more "elevated" planes of reference. The symbolism of darkness allows us to grasp its meaning not only in its cosmological and initiatory contexts (cosmic night, prenatal darkness, etc.), but also in the mystical experience of the "dark night of the soul" of St. John of the Cross. . . . But then one may ask if these "elevated" meanings were not in some manner implied in the other meanings, and if, as a consequence, they were, if not plainly understood, at least vaguely felt by men living on archaic levels of culture. This poses an important problem which unfortunately we cannot discuss here; how can one judge how far these "elevated" meanings of a symbol are fully known and realized by such and such an individual belonging to such and such a culture?" The difficulty of the problem rests in the fact that symbols address themselves not only to the awakened consciousness, but to the totality of the psychic life. Consequently, we do not have the right to conclude that the message of the symbols is confined to the meanings of which a certain number of individuals are fully conscious, even when we learn from a rigorous investigation of these individuals what they think of such and such a symbol belonging to their own tradition. Depth psychology has taught us that the symbol delivers its message and fulfills its function even when its meaning escapes awareness.

This admitted, two important consequences follow:

1. If at a certain moment in history a religious symbol has been able to express clearly a transcendent meaning, one is justified in supposing that this meaning might have been already grasped dimly at an earlier epoch.

2. In order to decipher a religious symbol, not only is it necessary to take into consideration all of its contexts, but one must above all reflect on the meanings that this symbol has had in what we might call its "maturity." Analyzing the symbolism of magic flight in a previous work, we came to the conclusion that it reveals dimly the ideas of "liberty" and of "transcendence," but that it is chiefly on the level of spiritual activity that the symbolism of flight and of ascension becomes completely intelligible. This is not to say that one must put all meanings of this symbolism on the same plane — from the flight of shamans to the mystical ascension. However, since the "cipher" constituted by this symbolism carries with it in its structure all the values that have been progressively revealed to man in the course of time, it is necessary in deciphering them to take into account their most general meaning, that is, the one meaning which can articulate all the other, particular meanings and which alone permits us to understand how the latter have formed a structure (Eliade 1959, 106–7).

2

The Depth Psychology of Carl Jung

Fifteen years later while I was researching the ethnology of the Sacred Pipe at the University of Aberdeen, Scotland, I began reading the depth psychology of Carl Jung. This experience made me aware of how deeply Native American religions, including the Sacred Pipe, touch the depths of the human psyche. It was the archetypes of what Jung called the collective unconscious that complemented Eliade's phenomenology in establishing a biological foundation for the common religious experience of humankind. Jung's depth psychology verified Eliade's observations. Jung gives precision to Eliade's treatment of the unconscious by his development of the collective unconscious and of the archetypes. In Jung's words:

There are present in every individual, besides his personal memories, the great "primordial" images . . . the inherited powers of human imagination as it was from time immemorial. The fact of this inheritance explains the truly amazing phenomenon that certain motifs from myths and legends repeat themselves the world over in identical forms. It also explains why it is that our mental patients can reproduce exactly the same images and associations that are known to us from the old texts. I give some examples of this in my book *Symbols of Transformation* (Jung 1953–86, 5). In so doing I do not by any means assert the inheritance of ideas, but only of the possibility of such ideas, which is something very different (Jung 1953–86, 7. ¶ 101).

In this further stage of treatment, then, when fantasies are produced which no longer rest on personal memories, we have to do with the manifestations of a deeper layer of the unconscious where the primordial images common to humanity lie sleeping. I have called these images or motifs, "archetypes," also "dominants" of the unconscious (Jung 1953–86, 7. ¶ 102). . . . This discovery means another step forward in our understanding: the recognition, that is, of two layers in the unconscious. We have to distinguish between a personal unconscious and an impersonal or transpersonal unconscious. We speak of the latter also as the collective unconscious, because it is detached from anything personal and is entirely universal, and because its contents can be found everywhere, which is naturally not the case with the personal contents. The personal unconscious contains lost memories, painful ideas that are repressed (i.e., forgotten on purpose), subliminal perceptions, by which are meant sense-perceptions that were not strong enough to reach consciousness, and finally, contents that are not yet ripe for consciousness. It corresponds to the figure of the shadow so frequently met with in dreams (Jung 1953–86, 7. ¶ 103).

The archetypes are part of human biological inheritance.

So this idea has been stamped on the human brain for aeons. That is why it lies ready to hand in the unconscious of every man. Only, certain conditions are needed to cause it to appear. . . . The greatest and best thoughts of man shape themselves' upon these primordial images as upon a blueprint. I have often been asked where the archetypes or primordial images come from. It seems to me that their origin can only be explained by assuming them to be deposits of the constantly repeated experiences of humanity. One of the commonest and at the same time most impressive experiences is the apparent movement of the sun every day. We certainly cannot discover anything of the kind in the unconscious, so far as the known physical process is concerned. What we do find, on the other hand, is the myth of the sun-hero in all its countless modifications. It is this myth, and not the physical process, that forms the sun archetype. The same can be said of the phases of the moon. The archetype is a kind of readiness to produce over and over again the same or similar mythical ideas. Hence it seems as though what is impressed upon the unconscious were exclusively the subjective fantasy-ideas aroused by the physical process. Therefore we may take it that archetypes are recurrent impressions made by subjective reactions. Naturally this assumption only pushes the problem further back without solving it. There is nothing to prevent us from assuming that certain archetypes exist even in animals, that they are grounded in the peculiarities of the living organism itself and are therefore direct expressions of life whose nature cannot be further explained. Not only are the archetypes, apparently, impressions of ever-repeated typical experiences, but, at the same time, they behave empirically like agents that tend towards the repetition of these same experiences. For when an archetype appears in a dream, in a fantasy, or in life, it always brings with it a certain influence or power by virtue of which it either exercises a numinous or a fascinating effect, or impels to action (Jung 1953–86, 7. ¶ 109):

Man "possesses" many things which he has never acquired but has inherited from his ancestors. He is not born as a *tabula rasa*, he is merely born unconscious. But he brings with him systems that are organized and ready to function in a specifically human way, and these he owes to millions of years of human development. Just as the migratory and nest-building instincts of birds were never learnt or acquired individually, man brings with him at birth the ground-plan of his nature, and not only of his individual nature but of his collective nature. These inherited systems correspond to the human situations that have existed since primeval times: youth and old age, birth and death, sons and daughters, fathers and mothers, mating, and so on. Only the individual consciousness experiences these things for the first time, but not the bodily system and the unconscious. For them they are only the habitual functioning of instincts that were preformed long ago (Jung 1953–86, 4. ¶ 728).

As the evolution of the embryonic body repeats its prehistory, so the mind grows up through the series of its prehistoric stages.

We receive along with our body a highly differentiated brain which brings with it its entire history, and when it becomes creative it creates out of this history — out of the history of mankind. By "history" we usually mean the history which we "make," and we call this "objective history." The truly creative fantasy activity of the brain has nothing to do with this kind of history, but solely with that age-old natural history which has been transmitted in living form since the remotest times, namely, the history of the brain-structure. And this structure tells its own story, which is the story of mankind: the unending myth of death and rebirth, and of the multitudinous figures who weave in and out of this mystery (Jung 1953–86, 10. ¶ 12).

Jung uses the models of the atom and the crystalline structure to give an insight into the nature of the archetype.

Whatever we say about the archetypes, they remain visualizations or concretizations which pertain to the field of consciousness. But we cannot speak about archetypes in any other way. We must, however, constantly bear in mind that what we mean by "archetype" is in itself irrepresentable, but has effects which make visualizations of it possible, namely, the archetypal images and ideas. We meet with a similar situation in physics: where the smallest particles are themselves irrepresentable but have effects from the nature of which we can build up a model. The archetypal image, the motif or mythologem, is a construction of this kind. . . . If on the basis of its observations psychology assumes the existence of certain irrepresentable psychoid factors, it is doing the same thing in principle as physics does when the physicist constructs an atomic model (Jung 1953–86, 8. ¶ 417).

A primordial image is determined as to its content only when it has become conscious and is therefore filled out with the material of conscious experience. Its form, however, as I have explained elsewhere, might perhaps be compared to the axial system of a crystal, which, as it were, preforms the crystalline structure in the mother liquid, although it has no material existence of its own. This first appears according to the specific way in which the ions and molecules aggregate. The archetype in itself is empty and purely formal, nothing but a *facultas praeformandi*, a possibility of representation which is given a priori. The representations themselves are not inherited, only the forms, and in that respect they correspond in every way to the instincts, which are also determined in form only. The existence of the instincts can no more be proved than the existence of the archetypes, so long as they do not manifest themselves concretely. With regard to the definiteness of the form, our comparison with the crystal is illuminating in as much as the axial system determines only the stereometric structure but not the concrete form of the individual crystal. This may be either large or small, and it may vary endlessly by reason of the different size of its planes or by the growing together of two crystals.

The only thing that remains constant is the axial system, or rather, the invariable geometric proportions underlying it. The same is true of the archetype. In principle, it can be named and has an invariable nucleus of meaning — but always only in principle, never as regards its concrete manifestation. In the same way, the specific appearance of the mother-image at any given time cannot be deduced from the mother archetype alone, but depends on innumerable other factors (Jung 1953–86, 9i. ¶ 155).

The archetypes are inborn forms of intuition related to the instincts.

Such cases [such as the yucca moth pollinating a plant once in its lifetime] are difficult to explain on the hypothesis of learning and practice. Hence other ways of explanation . . . have recently been put forward, laying stress on the factor of intuition. Intuition is an unconscious process in that its result is the irruption into consciousness of an unconscious content, a sudden idea or "hunch." It resembles a process of perception, but unlike the conscious activity of the senses and introspection the perception is unconscious. That is why we speak of intuition as an "instinctive" act of comprehension. It is a process analogous to instinct, with the difference that whereas instinct is a purposive impulse to carry out some highly complicated action, intuition is the unconscious, purposive apprehension of a highly complicated situation (Jung 1953–86, 8. ¶ 269).

In this "deeper" stratum we also find the a priori, in-

born forms of "intuition, namely the *archetypes* of perception and apprehension, which are the necessary a priori
determinants of all psychic processes. Just as his instincts
compel man to a specifically human mode of existence, so
the archetypes force his ways of perception and apprehension into specifically human patterns. The instincts and
the archetypes together form the "collective unconscious"
(Jung 1953–86, 8. ¶ 270).

*The archetype is the bridge between matter and spirit, between
psyche and the earth.*

Since psyche and matter are contained in one and the
same world, and moreover are in continuous contact with
one another and ultimately rest on irrepresentable, transcendental factors, it is not only possible but fairly probable, even, that psyche and matter are two different aspects
of one and the same thing (Jung 1953–86, 8. ¶ 418). . . .
the position of the archetype would be located beyond the
psychic sphere, analogous to the position of physiological
instinct, which is immediately rooted in the stuff of the
organism and, with its psychoid nature, forms the bridge
to matter in general. In archetypal conceptions and instinctual perceptions, spirit and matter confront one another on the psychic plane. Matter and spirit both appear
in the psychic realm as distinctive qualities of conscious
contents. The ultimate nature of both is transcendental,
that is, irrepresentable, since the psyche and its contents
are the only reality which is given to us *without a medium*
(Jung 1953–86, 8. ¶ 420).

Its contents, the archetypes, are as it were the hidden foundations of the conscious mind, or, to use another comparison, the roots which the psyche has sunk not only in the earth in the narrower sense but in the world in general. Archetypes are systems of readiness for action, and at the same time images and emotions. They are inherited with the brain structure — indeed, they are its psychic aspect. They represent, on the one hand, a very strong instinctive conservatism, while on the other hand they are the most effective means conceivable of instinctive adaptation. They are thus, essentially, the chthonic portion of the psyche, if we may use such an expression — that portion through which the psyche is attached to nature, or in which its link with the earth and the world appears at its most tangible. The psychic influence of the earth and its laws is seen most clearly in these primordial images (Jung 1953–86, 10. ¶ 53).

The archetypes are activated by human experience.

The original structural components of the psyche are of no less surprising a uniformity than are those of the visible body. The archetypes are, so to speak, organs of the prerational psyche. They are eternally inherited forms and ideas which have at first no specific content. Their specific content only appears in the course of the individual's life, when personal experience is taken up in precisely these forms. . . . I must content myself with the hypothesis of an omnipresent, but differentiated, psychic structure which is inherited and which necessarily gives a certain form and direction to all experience. For, just as the organs of the body are not mere lumps of indifferent, passive matter, but are dynamic, functional complexes which assert themselves with imperious urgency, so also the archetypes, as organs of the psyche, are dynamic, instinctual complexes which determine psychic life to an extraordinary degree. That is why I also call them dominants of the unconscious. The layer of unconscious psyche, which is made up of these universal dynamic forms I have termed the *collective unconscious* (Jung 1953–86, 11. ¶ 845).

The archetypes are charged with numinosity.

This illustrates the way in which archetypes appear in practical experience. In the first case they appear in their original form — they are images and at the same time emotions. One can speak of an archetype only when these two aspects coincide. When there is only an image, it is merely a word-picture, like a corpuscle with no electric charge. It is then of little consequence, just a word and nothing more. But if the image is charged with numinosity, that is, with psychic energy, then it becomes dynamic and will produce consequences. It is a great mistake in practice to treat an archetype as if it were a mere name, word, or concept. It is far more than that: it is a piece of life, an image connected with the living individual by the bridge of emotion. The word alone is a mere abstraction, an exchangeable coin in intellectual commerce. But the archetype is living matter. (Jung 1953–86, 18. ¶ 589).

The archetype as spirit opens humans to the transcendental.

Since we are psychic beings and not entirely dependent upon space and time, we can easily understand the
central importance of the resurrection idea: we are not
completely subjected to the powers of annihilation because our psychic totality reaches beyond the barrier of
space and time. Through the progressive integration of
the unconscious we have a reasonable chance to make
experiences of an archetypal nature providing us with the
feeling of continuity before and after our existence. The
better we understand the archetype, the more we participate in its life and the more we realize its eternity or
timelessness (Jung 1953–86, 18. ¶ 1572).

This unconscious, buried in the structure of the brain
and disclosing its living presence only through the medium of creative fantasy, is the *suprapersonal unconscious.* It
comes alive in the creative man, it reveals itself in the
vision of the artist, in the inspiration of the thinker, in the
inner experience of the mystic. The suprapersonal unconscious, being distributed throughout the brain-structure,
is like an all-pervading, omnipresent, omniscient spirit. It
knows man as he always was, and not as he is at this
moment; it knows him as myth. For this reason, also, the
connection with the suprapersonal or *collective* unconscious
means an extension of man beyond himself; it means death
for his personal being and a rebirth in a new dimension,
as was literally enacted in certain of the ancient mysteries.
It is certainly true that without the sacrifice of man as
he is, man as he was — and always will be — cannot be

attained. And it is the artist who can tell us most about this sacrifice of the personal man, if we are not satisfied with the message of the Gospels (Jung 1953–86, 10. ¶ 13).

The archetypes are part of a transconscious psyche.

The assumption that the human psyche possesses layers that lie *below* consciousness is not likely to arouse serious opposition. But that there could just as well be layers lying *above* consciousness seems to be a surmise which borders on a [crime against human majesty]. In my experience the conscious mind can claim only a relatively central position and must accept the fact that the tranconscious psyche transcends and as it were surrounds it on all sides. Unconscious contents connect it *backwards* with physiological states on the one hand and archetypal data on the other. But it is extended *forwards* by intuitions which are determined partly by archetypes and partly subliminal perceptions depending on the relativity of time and space in the unconscious (Jung 1953–86, 12. ¶ 175).

The importance of not losing contact with archetypal images.

This loss of instinct is largely responsible for the pathological condition of our contemporary culture. The great psychotherapeutic systems embodied in religion still struggle to keep the way open to the archetypal world of the psyche, but religion is increasingly losing its grip with

the result that much of Europe today has become dechris-
tianized or actually anti-Christian. Seen in this light, the
efforts of modern psychology to investigate the unconscious seem like salutary reactions of the European psyche, as if it were seeking to re-establish the connection
with its lost root. . . . It is not simply a matter of rescuing
the natural instincts (this seems to have been Freud's particular preoccupation), but of making contact again with
the archetypal functions that set bounds to the instincts
and give them form and meaning. For this purpose a
knowledge of the archetypes is indispensable (Jung
1953–86, 18. ¶ 1494).

*Jung's understanding of Christ as an archetypal image was an
important stage in my intellectual journey.*

The whole pre-Christian and Gnostic theology of the
Near East (some of whose roots go still further back)
wraps itself about him [Christ] and turns him before our
eyes into a dogmatic figure who has no more need of
historicity. At a very early stage, therefore, the real Christ
vanished behind the emotions and projections that
swarmed about him from far and near; immediately and
almost without trace he was absorbed into the sur-
rounding religious systems and molded into their archetypal exponent. He became the collective figure whom the
unconscious of his contemporaries expected to appear,
and for this reason it is pointless to ask who he "really"
was. Were he human and nothing else, and in this sense
historically true, he would probably be no more enlight-

ening a figure than, say, Pythagoras, or Socrates, or Apollonius of Tyana. He opened men's eyes to revelation precisely because he was, from everlasting, God, and therefore unhistorical; and he functioned as such only by virtue of the consensus of unconscious expectation. . . . At any rate the documentary reports relating to the general projection and assimilation of the Christ-figure are unequivocal. There is plenty of evidence for the cooperation of the collective unconscious in view of the abundance of parallels from the history of religion. In these circumstances we must ask ourselves what it was in man that was stirred by the Christian message, and what was the answer he gave (Jung 1953–86, 11. ¶ 228).

If we are to answer this psychological question, we must first of all examine the Christ-symbolism contained in the New Testament, together with the patristic allegories and medieval iconography, and compare this material with the archetypal content of the unconscious psyche in order to find out what archetypes have been constellated. The most important of the symbolical statements about Christ are those which reveal the attributes of the hero's life: improbable origin, divine father, hazardous birth, rescue in the nick of time, precocious development, conquest of the mother and of death, miraculous deeds, a tragic, early end, symbolically significant manner of death, post-mortem effects (reappearances, signs and marvels, etc.) (Jung 1953–86, 11. ¶ 229).

The archetype of the self made humans open to the Christian message.

It was this archetype of the self in the soul of every man that responded to the Christian message, with the result that the concrete Rabbi Jesus was rapidly assimilated by the constellated archetype. In this way Christ realized the idea of the self. But as one can never distinguish empirically between a symbol of the self and a God-image, the two ideas, however much we try to differentiate them, always appear blended together, so that the self appears synonymous with the inner Christ of the Johannine and Pauline writings, and Christ with God ("of one substance with the Father") (Jung 1953–86, 11. ¶ 231).

Incarnation appears as individuation on the human level.

The goal of psychological, as of biological, development is self-realization, or individuation. But since man knows himself only as an ego, and the self, as a totality, is indescribable and indistinguishable from a God-image, self-realization — to put it in religious or metaphysical terms — amounts to God's incarnation. . . . Through the Christ-symbol, man can get to know the real meaning of his suffering [involved in the individuation process]: he is on the way towards realizing his wholeness. As a result of the integration of conscious and unconscious, his ego enters the "divine" realm, where it participates in "God's suffering." The cause of the suffering is in both cases the same, namely "incarnation," which on the human level appears as "individuation". . . . The drama of the archetypal life of Christ describes in symbolic images the events in the conscious life — as well as in the life that transcends consciousness — of a man who has been transformed by his higher destiny (Jung 1953–86, 11. ¶ 233).

The psyche contains in itself the faculty for relationship with God.

Even the believing Christian does not know God's hidden ways and must leave him to decide whether he will work on man from outside or from within, through the soul. So the believer should not boggle at the fact that there are *somnia a Deo missa* (dreams sent by God) and illuminations of the soul which cannot be traced back to any external causes. It would be blasphemy to assert that God can manifest himself everywhere save only in the human soul. Indeed the very intimacy of the relationship between God and the soul precludes from the start any devaluation of the latter. It would be going perhaps too far to speak of an affinity; but at all events the soul must contain in itself the faculty of relationship to God, i.e., a correspondence, otherwise a connection could never come about. *This correspondence is, in psychological terms, the archetype of the God-image* (Jung 1953–86, 12. ¶ 11).

I have been accused of "deifying the soul." Not I but God himself has deified it. I did not attribute a religious function to the soul, I merely produced the facts which prove that the soul is *naturaliter religiosa,* [as Tertulian claimed] i.e., possesses a religious function. I did not invent or insinuate this function, it produces itself of its own accord without being prompted there to by any opinions or suggestions of mine. . . . For it is obvious that far too many people are incapable of establishing a connection between the sacred figures and their own psyche: they cannot see to what extent the equivalent images are lying dormant in their own unconscious (Jung 1953–86, 12. ¶ 14).

The unconscious, the source of the natural symbols found in primal religions, must be Christianized.

Every archetype is capable of endless development and differentiation. It is therefore possible for it to be more developed or less. In an outward form of religion where all the emphasis is on the outward figure (hence where we are dealing with a more or less complete projection), the archetype is identical with externalized ideas but remains unconscious as a psychic factor. When an unconscious content is replaced by a projected image to that extent, it is cut off from all participation in and influence on the conscious mind. Hence it largely forfeits its own life, because prevented from exerting the formative influence on consciousness natural to it; what is more, it remains in its original form unchanged, for nothing changes in the unconscious. At a certain point it even develops a tendency to regress to lower and more archaic levels. It may easily happen, therefore, that a Christian who believes in all the sacred figures is still undeveloped and unchanged in his inmost soul because he has "all God outside" and does not experience him in the soul. His deciding motives, his ruling interests and impulses, do not spring from the sphere of Christianity but from the unconscious and undeveloped psyche, which is as pagan and archaic as ever (Jung 1953–86, 12. ¶ 12).

God is an archetype of the unconscious.

In religious matters it is a well-known fact that we cannot understand a thing until we have experienced it inwardly, for it is in the inward experience that the connection between the psyche and the outward image or creed is first revealed as a relationship or correspondence like that of *sponsus and sponsa.* Accordingly when I say as a psychologist that God is an archetype, I mean by that the "type" in the psyche. The word "type" is, as we know, derived from τυπος, "blow" or "imprint"; thus an archetype presupposes an imprinter. Psychology as the science of the soul has to confine itself to its subject and guard against overstepping its proper boundaries by metaphysical assertions or other professions of faith. Should it set up a God, even as a hypothetical cause, it would have implicitly claimed the possibility of proving God, thus exceeding its competence in an absolutely illegitimate way (Jung 1953–86, 12. ¶ 15).

Jung, however, admits that psychology does not give a total understanding of reality, an admission saving his psychology from reductionism and implying the need for other disciplines.

These considerations have made me extremely cautious in my approach to the further metaphysical significance that may possibly underlie archetypal statements.

There is nothing to stop their ultimate ramifications from penetrating to the very ground of the universe. We alone are the dumb ones if we fail to notice it. Such being the case, I cannot pretend to myself that the object of archetypal statements has been explained and disposed of merely by our investigation of its psychological aspects. What I have put forward can only be, at best, a more or less successful or unsuccessful attempt to give the inquiring mind some access to one side of the problem — the side that can be approached [through psychological methods] (Jung 1953–86, 11. ¶ 295).

Although the archetypes are not restricted to Christianity, they are the foundation of Christian experience.

Now if my psychological researches have demonstrated the existence of certain psychic types and their correspondence with well-known religious ideas, then we have opened up a possible approach to those experienceable contents which manifestly and undeniably form the empirical foundations of all religious experience (Jung 1953–86, 12. ¶ 16). . . . It stands to reason that the expressions of the unconscious are natural and not formulated dogmatically; they are exactly like the patristic allegories which draw the whole of nature into the orbit of their amplifications. If these present us with some astonishing, *allegoriae Christi,* we find much the same sort of thing in the psychology of the unconscious. The only difference is that the patristic allegory *ad Christem spectat* — refers to Christ — whereas the psychic archetype is simply itself and can therefore be interpreted according to time, place, and milieu. In the West the archetype is filled out with the dogmatic figure of Christ; in the East, with Purusha, the Atman, Hiranyagarbha, the Buddha, and so on. The religions point of view, understandably enough, puts the accent on the imprinter, whereas scientific psychology emphasizes the *typos*, the imprint—the only thing it can understand. The religious point of view understands the imprint as the working, of an imprinter: the scientific point of view understands it as the symbol of an unknown and incomprehensible content. Since the *typos* is less definite and more variegated than any of the figures postulated by religion, psychology is compelled by its empirical material to express the *typos* by means of a terminology not bound by time, place, or milieu. If, for example, the *typos* agreed in every detail with the dogmatic figure of Christ, and if it contained no determinant that went beyond that figure, we would be bound to regard the *typos* as at least a faithful copy of the dogmatic figure, and to name it accordingly. The *typos* would then coincide with Christ. But as experience shows, this is not the case, seeing that the unconscious, like the allegories employed by the Church Fathers, produces countless other determinants that are not explicitly contained in the dogmatic formula; that is to say, non-Christian figures such as those mentioned above are included in the *typos*. But neither do these figures comply with the indeterminate nature of the archetype. It is altogether inconceivable that there could be any definite figure capable of expressing archetypal indefiniteness. For this reason I have found myself obliged to give the corresponding archetype the psychological name of the "self" — a term on the one hand definite enough to convey the essence of human wholeness and on the other hand indefinite enough to express the indescribable and indeterminable nature of this wholeness. The paradoxical qualities of the term are a reflection of the fact that wholeness consists partly of the conscious man and partly of the unconscious man. But we cannot define the latter or indicate his boundaries. Hence in its scientific usage the term "self" refers neither to Christ nor to the Buddha but to the totality of the figures that are its equivalent, and each of these figures is a symbol of the self. This mode of expression is an intellectual necessity in scientific psychology and in no sense denotes a transcendental prejudice. On the contrary, as we have said before. this objective attitude enables one man to decide in favor of the determinant Christ, another in favor of the Buddha, and so on (Jung 1953–86, 12. ¶ 20).

The Christ-symbol is of the greatest importance for psychology insofar as it is perhaps the most highly developed and differentiated symbol of the self, apart from the figure of the Buddha. We can see this from the scope and substance of all the pronouncements that have been made about Christ: they agree with the psychological phenomenology of the self in unusually high degree, although they do not include all aspects of this archetype [especially the shadow] (Jung 1953–86, 12. ¶ 22).

3

The Theology of Karl Rahner

Karl Rahner's concept of the supernatural existential, the anonymous Christian, Christ as part of the evolutionary process and the Christo-presence in creation established a theological foundation for my intellectual journey to understanding the Sacred Pipe as an archetypal image of Christ. Rahner starts by developing four theses concerning the relationship of Christianity to non-Christian religions. Although his starting point may seem to express triumphantism, he is very sensitive to the value of these religions and the need that Christianity has of them. In Rahner's words:

1st Thesis: This thesis states that Christianity understands itself as the absolute religion, intended for all men, which cannot recognize any other religion beside itself as of equal right. . . . Christianity [however] can recognize itself as the true and lawful religion for all men only where and when it enters with existential power and demanding force into the realm of another religion and — judging it by itself — puts it in question (Rahner 1961–91, 5:118).

[This will not happen if there is] the absence of any sufficient historical encounter with Christianity which would
have enough historical power to render the Christian religion really present in this pagan society and in the history
of the people concerned (Rahner 1961–91, 5:121).

2nd Thesis: The thesis itself is divided into two parts.
It means first of all that it is a priori quite possible to
suppose that there are supernatural, grace-filled elements
in non-Christian religions (Rahner 1961–91, 5:121). . . .
But God desires the salvation of everyone. And this salvation willed by God is the salvation won by Christ, the
salvation of supernatural grace which divinizes man, the
salvation of the beatific vision. It is a salvation really intended for all those millions upon millions of men who
lived perhaps a million years before Christ — and also for
those who have lived after Christ — in nations, cultures
and epochs of a very wide range which were still completely shut off from the viewpoint of those living in the
light of the New Testament (5:122–23). Our second thesis
goes even further than this, however, and states in its
second part that, from what has been said, the actual religions of "preChristian" humanity too must not be regarded as simply illegitimate from the very start, but must
be seen as quite capable of having a positive significance
(5:125).

In view of the social nature [and solidarity] of man . . .
it is quite unthinkable that man, being what he is, could
actually achieve this relationship to God . . . in an absolutely private interior reality and this outside of the actual
religious bodies which offer themselves to him in the envi-

ronment in which he lives. If man had to be and could always and everywhere be a *homo religiosus* in order to be able to save himself as such, then he was this *homo religiosus* in the concrete religion in which "people" lived and had to live at that time. . . . As already stated above, the inherence of the individual exercise of religion in a social religious order is one of the essential traits of true religion as it exists in practice (Rahner 1961–91, 5:128–29).

These traces [of God's grace in non-Christian religions] may be difficult to distinguish even to the enlightened eye of the Christian. But they must be there. And perhaps we may only have looked too superficially and with too little love at the non-Christian religions and so have not really seen them (Rahner 1961–91, 5:130).

3rd Thesis: If the second thesis is correct, then Christianity does not simply confront the member of an extra-Christian religion as a mere non-Christian but as someone who can and must already be regarded in this or that respect as an anonymous Christian. It would be wrong to regard the pagan as someone who has not yet been touched in any way by God's grace and truth . . . when he has already been given revelation in a true sense even before he has been affected by missionary preaching from without. For this grace, understood as the a priori horizon of all his spiritual acts, accompanies his consciousness subjectively, even though it is not known objectively. And the revelation which comes to him from without is not in such a case the proclamation of something as yet absolutely unknown, in the sense in which one tells a child here in Bavaria, for the first time in school, that there is a continent called Australia. Such a revelation is then the expression in objective concepts of something which this person has already attained or could already have attained in the depth of his rational existence (Rahner 1961–91, 5:131). . . . But if it is true that a person who becomes the object of the Church's missionary efforts is or may be already someone on the way towards his salvation, and someone who in certain circumstances finds it, without being reached by the proclamation of the Church's message — and if it is at the same time true that this salvation which reaches him in this way is Christ's salvation, since there is no other salvation — then it must be possible to be not only an anonymous theist [in the case of the atheist] but also an anonymous Christian (5:132).

4th Thesis: It is nevertheless absolutely permissible for the Christian himself to interpret this non-Christianity as Christianity of an anonymous kind which he does always still go out to meet as a missionary, seeing it as a world which is to be brought to the explicit consciousness of what already belongs to it as a divine offer or already pertains to it also over and above this as a divine gift of grace accepted unreflectedly and implicitly. If both these statements are true, then the Church will not so much regard herself today as the exclusive community of those who have a claim to salvation but rather as the historically tangible vanguard and the historically and socially constituted explicit expression of what the Christian hopes is present as a hidden reality even outside the visible Church (Rahner 1961–91, 5:133). Non-Christians may think it presumption for the Christian to judge everything which is sound or restored (by being sanctified) to be the fruit in every man of the grace of his Christ, and to interpret it as anonymous Christianity; they may think it presumption for the Christian to regard the non-Christian as a Christian who has not yet come to himself reflectively. But the Christian cannot renounce this 'presumption' which is really the source of the greatest humility for both himself and for the Church (5:134).

Man has a supernatural existential that finds its fulfillment in Christ.

This self-communication by God offered to all and fulfilled in the highest way in Christ rather constitutes the goal of all creation and — since God's word and will *effect* what they say — that, even before he freely takes up an attitude to it, it stamps and determines man's nature and lends it a character which we may call a "supernatural existential". A refusal of this offer would therefore not leave man in a state of pure unimpaired nature, but would bring him into contradiction with himself even in the sphere of his own being. This means positively that man in experiencing his transcendence, his limitless openness — no matter how implicit and incomprehensible it always is — also already experiences the offer of grace — not necessarily expressly as grace, as a distinctly supernatural calling, but experiences the reality of its content. But this means that the express revelation of the word in Christ is not something which comes to us from without as entirely strange, but only the explicitation of what we already are by grace and what we experience at least incoherently in the limitlessness of our transcendence. The expressly Christian revelation becomes the explicit statement of the revelation of grace which man always experiences implicitly in the depths of his being (Rahner 1961–91, 6:393–94).

If man accepts the revelation, he posits by that fact the act of supernatural faith. But he also already accepts this revelation whenever he really accepts himself completely, for it already speaks in him. Prior to the explicitness of official ecclesiastical faith this acceptance can be present in an implicit form (Rahner 1961–91, 6:394).

This supernatural existential exists in the depths of man's nature and makes salvation history coexistent with human history, reaching a climax in Christ.

The divine self-bestowal (at least as offered and bestowed upon the free creature as that which makes it possible for it to act for its own salvation) penetrates to the ultimate roots of man's being, to the innermost depths of his spiritual nature, and takes effect upon him from there, radically re-orientating this nature of his towards the immediate presence of God. It imparts to this nature an inward dynamism and an ultimate tendency towards God himself that is a grace. . . . This "supernatural existential" or mode of being (as we may call this finality and dynamic impulse which makes us tend towards the immediate presence of God) is indeed the outcome of grace. But it is inserted into man's nature through the salvific will of God to become an abiding element in his spiritual mode of being, and as something that is a living force in man always and everywhere, whether accepted or rejected by man's own free will. It radically influences the ultimate development of his existence as spiritual (Rahner 1961–91, 10:34–35).

Thus the presence of the abiding "supernatural existential" in man has the effect of making saving history coexistent with human history in general in its spiritual dimension, even though in many cases man himself does not consciously advert to this or formulate to himself what is taking place in this spiritual dimension. To this extent we can and must say that either saving history or its opposite, the history of perdition, is taking place wherever man of his own free decision either voluntarily undertakes his own mode of existence or alternatively protests against it. And this is precisely because this "supernatural existential," considered as God's act of self-bestowal which he offers to men, is in all cases grafted into the very roots of human existence" (Rahner 1961–91, 10:36).

The relationship between the supernatural existential and human nature is not something merely extrinsic but truly intrinsic.

[If grace is merely extrinsic] supernatural grace then can only be the superstructure lying beyond the range of experience imposed upon a human "nature" which even in the present economy turns in its own orbit. . . . Hence this nature [would only be] first of all merely "disturbed" by the purely external "decree" of God commanding the acceptance of the supernatural, a decree which continues to be a purely exterior divine ordination so long as grace has not yet laid hold of this nature, justifying and divinizing it, and has in this way made the vocation to the supernatural end into man's inner goal (Rahner 1961–91 1:299).

Man should be able to receive this Love which is God himself; he must have a congeniality for it. He must be able to accept it (and hence grace, the beatific vision) as one who has room and scope, understanding and desire for it. Thus he must have a real "potency" for it. He must have it always. He is indeed someone always addressed and claimed by this Love. For, as he now in fact is, he is created for it; he is thought and called into being so that Love might bestow itself. To this extent this "potency" is what is inmost and most authentic in him, the centre and root of what he is absolutely. . . . The capacity for the God of self-bestowing personal Love is the central and abiding existential of man as he really is (Rahner 1961–91, 1:311–12).

Although Rahner makes grace intrinsic to nature, it is still not owed to nature, remaining God's free gift.

Hence there is no longer any reason why speculative theology should avoid considering the relationship between the supernatural (including the supernatural existential) and nature in itself. . . . The spiritual nature will have to be such that it has an openness for this supernatural existential without thereby of itself demanding it unconditionally. This openness is not to be thought of merely as a non-repugnance, but as an inner ordination, provided only that it is not unconditional. It will be permissible at this point to point unhesitatingly at the unlimited dynamism of the spirit, which . . . is the natural existential immediately ordered to grace itself. . . . And one will guard against asserting that this natural dynamism is an unconditional demand for grace (Rahner 1961–91, 1:315).

Spirit, that is, openness for God, freedom and conscious self-possession, is essentially impossible without a transcendence whose absolute fulfillment is grace. Still, a fulfillment of this sort is not owed to it, if we suppose that this conscious possession of self in freedom before God is meaningful in itself, and not just as a pure means and a mere state of the way to beatific vision. This supposition arises from the absolute (not "infinite") value and validity of every personal act, in itself. If it be granted, it follows that there can be no spirit without a transcendence open to the supernatural; but spirit is meaningful, without supernatural grace. Hence its fulfillment in grace cannot be demanded by its essence, though it is open for such grace (Rahner 1961–91, 4:186).

The Church itself reaches its fulfillment by absorbing whatever is good in non-Christian religions.

This divine dynamism, then, latent in the entire history of the human spirit, transforms it into saving history and revelation history. And in doing this it impels this whole spiritual and religious history towards that point at which it becomes explicitly apprehensible as the history and manifestation of Christ and of his Church. And even though this point may lie in a future that is remote and invisible, it is in fact ultimately identical with the end of history and the return of Christ in glory. This is the first point. The second point is that Christianity and the Church themselves have only arrived at their definitive fullness and historical maturity when the whole of salvation history and revelation history has visibly and explicitly been transformed into the history of Christianity and of the Church and has become a definable element in the Christianity that is explicitly embodied in the Church. So far we have been treating of two basic principles, and in the light of the synthesis which we have achieved between them it now becomes intelligible to us that even Christianity and the Church themselves are constantly in process of seeking the final perfection of their own nature. And because of this they are in a position to recognise in those tendencies within the spiritual and religious history of mankind which are religiously positive even though not yet explicitly Christian, that which Christianity and the Church must absorb and transform into themselves in order to become fully that which they already are: the manifestation in history of the grace of God now at its eschatological stage in history and in a state of purity which is divinely attested and assured (Rahner 1961–91, 10:40).

The supernatural existential impelling all men and women to God is present in non-Christian religions.

When we reflect upon what we have already said at an earlier stage with regard to the "supernatural existential" present in every man in all ages, and with regard to the fact that the supernatural history of salvation and revelation are coexistent with the history of the human spirit, then it will become immediately comprehensible that the religions which de facto do exist outside Christianity and the Old Testament are not merely the outcome of human speculation, human wickedness or a self-willed decision on man's part to devise a religion for himself instead of accepting it from God. Instead of this the "supernatural existential," the dynamic impulse present in man by the power of grace and impelling him towards the triune God, is at work in all these religions and plays a decisive part in determining the forms in which these religions are objectively expressed (Rahner 1961–91, 10:46).

The success of missionary preaching presupposes the presence of an anonymous Christianity in non-Christian religions.

First we may surely say that in order to be possible or to have any hope of success missionary preaching necessarily presupposes that which we may call by the name of anonymous Christianity or by some other name. On any right understanding of the nature of the Christian faith it is clear that a missionary preaching is possible only if we presuppose the grace of faith (at least as offered). The word of God as preached can only be heard and received as the word of God through this grace of faith (Rahner 1961–91, 12:169). . . . The grace of faith is the necessary prior condition for the teaching of the faith. But it would be to suppose the miraculous, almost to indulge in mythological ideas, if we were to hold that this grace of faith was conferred only at that moment at which the preaching of the gospel actually reached the ears of those to whom it was addressed. In this moment it does indeed become actual, effective and demanding, but this is precisely in virtue of the fact that it has been present all along and belongs to the enduring existential modalities of man, albeit at the level of the supernatural, in the same way as the natural spiritual faculties are present all along in man even though they only become actual and effective when they encounter an external object of experience which corresponds to them (Rahner 1961–91, 12:170). . . . The missionary task, therefore, must be one that can exist together with anonymous Christianity because on theological grounds we must hold that this missionary task presupposes the existence of the anonymous Christian as the only possible hearer of the gospel message (12:171).

Admittedly in this connection [the need for a non-Christian to have true faith in salvation] there is actually a particular example to be mentioned: a Japanese who is a student chaplain in Japan has told me that the theory put forward here constitutes the indispensable condition for him such that it is only on this condition that he can perform his missionary work, precisely because he can then appeal to the anonymous Christian in the pagan and not simply seek to indoctrinate him with a teaching *ab externo* (Rahner 1961–91, 14:292–93).

If grace is present before the sacrament of baptism, it can also be present before the preaching of the word.

We have already emphasized above that on the occasion of the baptism of Cornelius Peter insists upon the fact that Cornelius can and indeed must be baptized *because* he has already received the Holy Spirit (Rahner 1961–91, 12:171). Even in baptism, then, the situation is that through it an anonymous Christian becomes an explicit Christian, and in any case through such a baptism he may indeed be validly baptized, but not justified. In the case of adult baptism the justification is prior to the baptism itself, and it is precisely in baptism that it achieves its manifestation at the ecclesiastical and social level. This does not entail any denial the efficacy of the sacrament as conferring grace, or make it impossible (12:172–73).

What is so much taken for granted in all the traditional theology concerning the relationship between grace and sacrament can unhesitatingly be extended to the relationship between grace and the word. . . . The explicit preaching of faith is not superfluous, because the grace which is preached is prior to this preaching as the condition of it and as the content of its preaching (Rahner 1961–91, 12:174).

The object of missionary activity is to incarnate Christ in non-Christian religions.

A positive evaluation of the meaning of mission is both possible along these lines, and in a true sense already given in what has been said so far. The grace of God which is intended effectively to redeem all has an incarnational character. It wills to extend itself into all the dimensions of human life, and in other words to take effect and find expression in the historical and social dimensions of this as well. This grace is intended of its very nature to be constitutive of the Church. Mission and the missionary actively contribute to this incarnational dynamism of grace . . . in the light of the missionary decree of the Second Vatican Council by the insight that mission is directed not exclusively to the individual in his own personal quest for salvation, but no less primarily to peoples and civilizations as such. Mission consists in a sending out to all people which has the task in saving history of making Christ, his gospel and his grace present among all peoples as such in their own specific histories and cultures, and thereby of achieving a quite new incarnational presence of Christ himself in the world. Once and for all Christianity is not intended merely to assure a salvation conceived of embryonically and almost in abstract terms for the individual in the other-worldly dimension, but is rather intended to make God's grace manifest here below in all its possible forms and in all historical spheres and contexts. The palpable dimension of the present world itself is intended to be made Christian to the utmost possible extent, because it is precisely not merely the other world that belongs to God and his Christ, as though he secretly rescued a few isolated individuals out of a merely secular world. On the contrary this world too belongs to him, the earthly dimension, history, the peoples, and also the history which present-day humanity itself sets itself actively to shape, instead of merely passively enduring it (Rahner 1961–91, 12:176). The declaration [of the Second Vatican Council] recognizes what is "true" and "holy" in the different religions and that the concrete forms and doctrines of these religions are to be regarded with straightforward seriousness. The declaration sees the ultimate root of these religions in the quest for an answer to the unsolved riddle of human existence and in a certain perception and acknowledgment of that hidden power which is present in the course of the world and in the events of human life. In a word, the council invites us to take seriously the non-Christian religions as such (Rahner 1961–91, 18:289).

Although there is a distinction between salvation history as a whole and the history of explicit Christianity, they are intimately related.

This optimism with regard to salvation remains one of the most astonishing phenomena in the development of the Church's conscious awareness of her faith in this development as it applies to the secular and non-Christian world, the awareness of the difference between saving history as a whole and the history of explicit Christianity and of the Church (Rahner 1961–91, 14:286). . . . A distinction is drawn between two factors: an original event of revelation consisting in the self-communication of God as addressed to all in virtue of his universal will to save and taking place at a preconceptual level in the roots of man's spiritual faculties on the one hand, and the objectification at the historical and conceptual level of this revelatory self-communication of God in that which we call revelation and the history of revelation in a more normal sense on the other (14:293).

There must be a Christian theory to account for the fact that every individual who does not in any absolute or ultimate sense act against his own conscience can say and does say in faith, hope and love, Abba within his own spirit, and is on these grounds in all truth a brother to Christians in God's sight. This is what the theory of the anonymous Christian seeks to say, and, insofar as it is valid, what it implies (Rahner 1961–91, 14:294).

There should be a mutual contribution between the systematic theologian and the historian of religions.

Here the systematic theologian must stop and hand over the question to the historian of religion working on experience. . . . The systematic theologian might, for example, ask the historian of religion if he cannot discover in a concrete and religious form those "sacraments of nature" which the dogmatic theologian postulates in the abstract and acknowledges as important for salvation. He could offer the empiricist fundamental insights perhaps revealing in and under an apparently solid polytheism a genuine relationship to the absolute God. He could show him that it is not a priori forbidden to discover genuine supernatural mysticism in the "mysticism" of religions of higher cultures, even when this extra-Christian "mysticism" is not itself by any means thematicized in an explicitly religious form (Rahner 1961–91, 18:295).

The supernatural existential reaching its climax in Christ has an evolutionary history that can be understood as matter attaining spirit through self-transcendence.

Without separating them from each other, we have tried to understand spirit and matter as two correlated elements of the one man, elements which are inseparable from each other and yet are not reducible to each other. . . . [But] this difference of nature must not be misunderstood to mean that these two elements are opposed in nature or absolutely different in nature or indifferent to each other. Starting from this inner interrelation between these two factors and concentrating on the temporal duration of this relationship between these two factors, it may be said without scruple that matter develops out of its inner being in the direction of the spirit. . . . [True "becoming"] must be understood as a real self-transcendence, a surpassing of self (Rahner 1961–91, 5:164). . . . This self-transcendence cannot be thought of in any other way than as an event which takes place by the power of the absolute fullness of being [God]. On the one hand, this absolute fullness of being must be thought of as something so *interior* to the finite being moving towards its fulfillment that the finite being is empowered by it to achieve a really active self-transcendence and does not merely receive this new reality passively as something effected by God. . . . Let us simply remark in this connection that this notion of self-transcendence includes also transcendence into what is substantially new, i.e. the leap to a higher *nature*. To exclude the latter would mean emptying the notion of self-transcendence of its content; it would mean that one could no longer evaluate certain phenomena with an untroubled mind, e.g. such notions as the procreation of a new human being by the parents in what appears at first sight to be a merely biological event. An essential self-transcendence, however, is no more an intrinsic contradiction than (simple) self-transcendence, as soon as one allows it to occur in the dynamism of the power of the absolute being which is within the creature and yet is not proper to its nature — in other words, — in what in theological language is called God's conservation of the creature and his concurrence with its activity (Rahner 1961–91, 5:165–66).

The boundary between matter and spirit cannot be precisely determined.

It is clear that the lower always moves slowly towards the boundary line in its history which it then crosses in its actual self-transcendence — that boundary line which is only seen to have been clearly crossed from the vantage point of a clearer development of the new condition, without it being possible however to give an absolutely clear definition of this line itself. Of course, these are all very abstract and vague statements. Naturally, it would in itself be desirable to show more concretely what common traits are to be found in the evolution of material, living and spiritual beings — to show (more exactly) how the merely material is a prelude in its own dimensions to the higher dimension of life, and how the latter in its dimension is a prelude to the spirit in its ever greater advance towards the border line to be crossed by self-transcendence (Rahner 1961–91, 5:167).

The cosmos becomes self-conscious in each individual person.

Hence one cannot say (especially when one bears in mind the uniqueness of each act of freedom) that this cosmic self-consciousness need not be given in man or can be given only once. It occurs each time, in its own unique way, in each individual man. The one material cosmos is, as it were, the *one* body of the *multifarious* [i.e., occurring in great variety] self-presence of this self-same cosmos and of its orientation to its absolute and infinite foundation. . . . For in his corporeality, every man is an element of the cosmos which cannot really be delimited and cut off from it, and in this corporeality he communicates with the whole cosmos in such a way that through this corporeality of man taken as the other element of belonging to the spirit, the cosmos really presses forward to this self-presence in the spirit (Rahner 1961–91, 5:170).

The angels are part of the cosmic evolution.

Furthermore, the theological data (into which we need not enter here in detail) show that the history even of the angels and the history of the world are at least interlaced in many respects. The common goal of both is the eternal kingdom of God; the granting of grace to men as citizens of the material world and to the angels is the same; in the Christian teaching the angels, whether they are to be thought of as good or bad, certainly exercise functions in this world; in particular, since they reach down to or into the material world, these functions must ultimately be based in the nature of the angels; the angels can be understood quite correctly, even according to scripture, as cosmic (even though personal) powers of the order of nature and of its history; Christian theology has always seen the object of the personal decision of personal spiritual powers, called angels, to lie in Christ and in his salvific function for the history of mankind and hence of the material world. If one looks at these data, it will be quite legitimate to be of the opinion that, first of all, the doctrine of the angels understood as 'pure spirits', no matter how materially correct, unjustifiably lends too much support to a platonic and non-Christian removal of the created spirit from this world. Furthermore, it will have to be said that the angels, in spite of their differences from man, can be conceived in such a way that, in their own way and of their own most proper and original nature, they are powers of the one and hence also material world to whose material nature they are genuinely and essentially related (Rahner 1961–91, 6:159).

God is intrinsic to the cosmic evolution.

The world receives God, the Infinite and the ineffable mystery, to such an extent that he himself becomes its innermost life. The concentrated, always unique self-possession of the cosmos in each individual spiritual person, and in his transcendence towards the absolute ground of his reality, takes place when this absolute ground itself becomes directly interior to that which is grounded by it. . . . If the history of the cosmos is always basically a spiritual history — the desire to become conscious of itself and of its cause — then the direct relationship to God in his self-communication to his spiritual creature, and in it to the cosmos in general as the goal which corresponds to the meaning of this development, is basically an indisputable fact (Rahner 1961–91, 5:172).

Jesus as human is part of cosmic evolution.

In the first place, the Saviour is himself a historical moment in God's saving action exercised on the world. He is a moment of the history of God's communication of himself to the world — in the sense that he is a part of this history of the cosmos itself. He must not be merely God acting on the world but must be a part of the cosmos itself in its very climax. This is in fact stated in the Christian dogma: Jesus is true man; he is truly a part of the earth, truly a moment in the biological evolution of this world, a moment of human natural history, for he is born of woman; he is a man who in his spiritual, human and finite subjectivity is just like us, a receiver of that self-communication of God by grace which we affirm of all men — and hence of the cosmos — as the climax of development in which the world comes absolutely into its own presence and into the direct presence of God (Rahner 1961–91, 5:176).

The Incarnation is the fulfillment of the divine plan of creation.

It should be stated, first of all, that there is quite a long established school of thought among Catholic theologians (usually called the "Scotist school") which has always stressed that the first and most basic motive for the Incarnation was not the blotting-out of sin but that the Incarnation was already the goal of the divine freedom even apart from any divine fore-knowledge of freely incurred guilt. This School holds therefore that — seen as the free climax of God's self-expression and self-effacement into the otherness of the creature — the Incarnation is the most original act of God anticipating the will to create and (presupposing sin) to redeem, by including them, as it were, as two of its moments (Rahner 1961–91, 5:184). . . . In the Catholic Church it is freely permitted to see the Incarnation first of all, in God's primary intention, as the summit and height of the divine plan of creation, and not primarily and in the first place as the act of a mere restoration of a divine world-order destroyed by the sins of mankind, an order which God had conceived in itself without any Incarnation (Rahner 1961–91, 5:185).

Christ achieves a cosmic presence through His incarnation and resurrection.

Again on the basis of this unity between spirit and matter it also becomes clearer for christology why the assumption of a spirit-creaturely reality by the Logos actually constitutes a hypostatic union with matter, an Incarnation of the Logos in the true sense, which attains to and commits itself to matter itself as such — in other words the radical potentiality of the world as such — and why the total reality of the world is ipso facto touched to its very roots by the Incarnation of the Logos precisely in virtue of the fact that matter must be conceived of fundamentally and from the outset as one (Rahner 1961–91, 11:219). . . . In a transcendental christology of this kind, as fitted into the totality of an evolutionary view of the world, the Christ-event is not something which is enacted upon a sort of cosmic stage which is static and unaffected by what is taking place in him, but rather constitutes the point to which the becoming of the world in its history is from the outset striving to attain (11:227). . . . it must further be said that we are not viewing the Christ-event in Jesus of Nazareth in a way that is in conformity with its true meaning and essence unless we bear in mind two factors: the First and Second Coming of the Incarnate Logos must be understood as a unity, as a single event still in process of achieving its fullness, such that in it the Life, Death and Resurrection of Jesus constitute merely the first beginning of an event which will only have achieved its fullness and definitive state when the world as a whole is illumined by, and brought face to face with, the immediacy of God, and in this sense when Jesus himself will have "come again." This in itself implicitly contains the second point which has to be borne in mind: Christ can only rightly be understood if in him the "head and body" which is the Church, and ultimately the world itself, are apprehended in their unity as constituting the one and whole Christ (Rahner 1961–91, 11:228).

Jesus' corporeal humanity is a permanent part of the one world with its single dynamism, a relation and unity which need closer examination. Consequently Jesus' resurrection is not only in the ideal order an "exemplary cause" of the resurrection of all, but objectively is the beginning of the transfiguration of the world as an ontologically interconnected occurrence. In this beginning the destiny of the world is already in principle decided and has already begun. At all events it would in reality be different if Jesus were not risen.

On the basis of these reflections systematic theology might then show why Jesus as pledge and beginning of the perfect fulfillment of the world, as representative of the new cosmos, as dispenser of the Spirit, head of the Church, dispenser of the sacraments (above all in the Eucharist), as heavenly mediator and goal of hope, can only be fully grasped if he is known throughout as the risen Lord, and if his resurrection is not thought of as his private destiny after a work which alone had soteriological significance. It would also appear that the risen Lord, freed by resurrection from the limiting individuality of the unglorified body, has in truth become present to the world precisely because risen (and so by his "going"), and that therefore his return will only be the disclosure of this relation to the world attained by Jesus in his resurrection (Rahner 1969, 333).

Intuitive Identifications

After reading Rahner, I felt a need to bring together the thinking of some thirty years. I made identifications through the process of intuition. Intuitions are not the result of reasoning. They cannot be proven but are accepted if they "click," that is lead to a new and more mature understanding.

I pondered the relationship between Jung's depth psychology and Eliade's phenomenology. In a careful analysis Mac Linscott Ricketts, (1970) states that although no simple equation can be made between Jung and Eliade, there are close parallels, especially when Eliade talks about the unconscious and the nature of symbolism as in the previous quotations.

Eliade's meeting with Jung at the Eranos conference at Ascona in 1950 did influence his thinking. His comments about the unconscious in his *The Sacred and the Profane* written after that meeting reflect that influence. Eliade and Jung, however, did not always use the term *archetype* to denote the same meaning. When Eliade spoke about the archetypal significance of mandala images from South Asian yogic contexts in his then new book on yoga, quoting Jung in support, Jung thought the difference was so great that it "seems nearly to have destroyed the personal friendship between the two men" (Miller 1995, 106–7).

What, then, is the primary relationship between Jung and Eliade? As stated earlier, Eliade's phenomenology is an amplification of Jung's archetypes. Eliade explains the common structure of religious experience on a concept of a transconscious rather than the collective unconscious. He states that "the Images provide 'openings' into a transhistorical world (24). . . . For it is through symbols that man finds his way out of his particular situation and 'opens' himself to the general and the universal" (13).* But Eliade sees a relationship between the unconscious and the transconscious. He admits that there are "nonhistorical expressions of the same archetypal symbolism, as found in religions, manifesting themselves in a coherent and systematic manner on the plane of the unconscious, as well as upon those of the trans-conscious." Those in the unconscious "present values, and a structure, that are in perfect agreement with those of the conscious manifestations" (15). Eliade wishes to interpret symbols on the transconscious rather than the unconscious plane. For Eliade the symbols should not be reduced to psychological data; rather they disclose their truest meaning when interpreted in the light of their highest expressions, namely, as

---

* The page numbers are cross-references within this volume.

intense religious experience and as exalted metaphysical philosophy.

Jung, however, despite his unwillingness as a psychologist to validate external reality, treats the same reality from the side of the psyche as Eliade from that of historical manifestations by proposing layers of the unconscious lying above consciousness as well as below. "The conscious mind . . . must accept the fact that the transconscious psyche transcends and as it were surrounds it on all sides" (39). Unconscious contents connect the conscious backward with archetypal data, on the one hand, and intuition extends it forward into a transconscious, on the other hand. He calls this a suprapersonal unconscious, which is an extension of a human beyond himself or herself. I believe that Eliade and Jung are describing the same reality from the points of view of two different disciplines.

Religious experience, then, can be interpreted in both directions, both higher and lower. Eliade has interpreted it on the higher level. But it can also be interpreted on the lower level without psychological reduction because the archetypes are pure forms that need activation from the natural symbols found in primal religions and so well documented by Eliade. When this is done, Eliade's phenomenological method becomes an amplification of the Jungian archetypes.

Jung and Eliade also helped me understand Rahner's theology. Rahner needs a depth psychology as well as a philosophy as a foundation of his theology precisely because he makes grace intrinsic to nature. He needs it to understand in the concrete what he is describing abstractly. Depth psychology, however, also needs theology for one to understand the nature of the psyche one is observing because it is a psyche influenced by grace. Pure depth psychology is a remainder concept — what would have been if grace had not been offered. (Pure theology is also a remainder concept — what would have been if grace were not intrinsic to nature.)

Rahner himself recognizes the need for the historian of religions and, one can add, the phenomenologist to understand theological questions and "to discover in a concrete and religious form those 'sacraments of nature' which the dogmatic theologian postulates in the abstract" (64). Jung's depth psychology and Eliade's phenomenology validate Rahner's theology, especially his concept of the anonymous Christian and the supernatural existential, a validation that theological discussion alone cannot make.

The concept of the anonymous Christian rests upon the presence of a tendency within humans toward the immediate presence of God, which Rahner calls a "supernatural existential." When humans experience this, they are already experiencing God's grace of self-bestowal. This supernatural existential is human spiritual nature, which has an openness to this presence (without thereby of itself demanding it unconditionally) elevated by a new final cause. Rahner sometimes uses the term *horizon,* instead of *final cause.* Jung is talking about this same reality when he says that "the soul must contain in itself the faculty of relationship to God, i.e. a correspondence, otherwise a connection could never come about" (43).

Jung's faculty of relationship to God is Rahner's spiritual nature that is open to God's grace. Jung's connection, which is the archetypal movement toward wholeness, is Rahner's spiritual nature becoming a supernatural existential. Eliade touches on this same reality in quoting Fr. Beirnaert, "How, moreover, could the candidates for baptism understand the symbolic images put before them if these did not respond to their obscure expectations?" (19). In other words, Jung was observing a psyche elevated by grace without being aware of it.

In the human unconscious is an archetype of the self that is the source of the human tendency toward wholeness (and transcendence because the archetypes have a transcendental quality that extends humans beyond themselves by means of intuitions). When it is activated by the proper existential experience, which in this case is God's gift of self-bestowal, it produces the archetypal image of the self. Jung calls this the process of individuation. The archetype of the self in the unconscious, elevated by grace, is in Rahner's terms the supernatural existential, which "penetrates to the ultimate roots of man's being. [it is] inserted into man's nature [i.e., into the archetypal tendency to wholeness] . . . to become an abiding element in his spiritual mode of being, and as something that is a living force in man always" (54–55). This abiding potency for the immediate presence of God is the archetype ready to be activated by the offer of self-bestowal. Rahner claims that a human "already accepts this revelation when he accepts himself completely, for it already speaks in him"

(54). But a human accepts himself completely only in the process of individuation by assimilating the contents of the unconsciousness into consciousness through which, according to Jung, "the ego enters the divine realm" (42). This potency must be more than an intellectual potency, something merely rational on the conscious level. Individuation can be seen as involving implicit faith in God's transcendence.

Rahner says that one should point "at the unlimited dynamism of the spirit which . . . is the natural existential immediately ordered to grace itself" (57). Jung gives the archetypal source of this dynamism. "One can speak of an archetype only when these two aspects [image and emotion] coincide. When there is only an image, it is merely a word picture, like a corpuscle with no electric charge. It is then of little consequence, just a word and nothing more. But if the image is charged with numinosity, that is, with psychic energy, then it becomes dynamic and will produce consequences" (37). One cannot separate the dynamism of spiritual nature from that of the archetype because matter and spirit cannot be separated. Rahner states that they are "two correlated elements of the one man, elements which are inseparable from each other" (65). For Jung, "since psyche and matter are contained in one and the same world, and moreover are in continuous contact with one another and ultimately rest on irrepresentable, transcendental factors, it is not only possible, but fairly probable, even, that psyche and matter are two different aspects of one and the same thing" (35). The archetype of the self that is always present in the human unconscious is the source of that living force waiting to be activated by God's offer of self-bestowal.

One of the chief theological objections against Rahner's position is that if the openness to God's immediate presence is intrinsic to humans, it must either be demanded, which is contrary to the notion of grace, or be a natural desire frustratable without grace, which is contrary to the notion of nature. Theologian Kenneth Eberhard comments:

Rahner's solution is simply to declare that the orientation itself is meaningful (as the condition for the possibility of man's thinking and willing) regardless of whether it achieves its final end or not. But is this true? Rahner cannot prove it. He must suppose that it is true, otherwise he is at a loss to explain the possibility of grace, and hence of the supernatural existential. One could argue here that Rahner's supposition is a shaky one at best. The fact that man's relationship to the absolute allows him to think and to be free is indeed a fulfillment. But is it an absolute fulfillment? Nothing but an absolute fulfillment will adequately solve the problem of natural desire. (1971, 561)

By viewing the supernatural existential as the archetypal movement of wholeness elevated by grace this dilemma can be avoided. The archetype is not determined by any one actuation. The indeterminate nature of the archetype means that no one definite actuation can express its indefiniteness. The archetype can be actuated either by the natural goal of knowing and willing or by the immediate presence of God by grace. This means that if humans had not been given the immediate presence of God as a goal, their natural desire, or archetypal tendency, would not have been frustrated. An archetypal tendency does not need its highest actuation to avoid frustration. Each actuation fulfills the archetypal movement whether it is a partial fulfillment on a natural level or an absolute fulfillment on the level of grace. Jungian depth psychology justifies Rahner's supposition that nature does not need an absolute fulfillment by grace to avoid frustration.

Rahner's supernatural existential is also verified by Eliade's phenomenology.

Whenever a tree incarnates the World Tree or when a spade is associated with the phallus and agricultural work with the act of generation, for example, one could say that the immediate reality of these objects or actions "bursts" or "explodes" under the irruptive force of a more profound reality. . . . Consequently, because of the symbol, the individual experience is awakened and transmuted in a spiritual act. To "live" a symbol and to decipher its message correctly implies an opening toward the Spirit and, finally, access to the universal [and ultimately to God's self-bestowal of Himself]. (12–13)

It is through symbols that a human, in Rahner's words, "in experiencing his transcendence, his limitless openness —no matter how implicit and incomprehensible it always is — also already experiences the offer of grace" (53). Pure phenomenology is also a remainder concept, what would have been without grace.

The supernatural existential, then, is an archetypal openness to transcendence, a part of human spiritual nature that has been elevated to a new orientation toward the immediate presence of God through final causality. Because of this openness, a human is implicitly oriented to Christ and is in Rahner's terms an anonymous Christian. Jung's discussion of Buddha and Christ as archetypal images gives valuable insights into this concept.

The grace of the supernatural existential is present in Buddha as well as Christ because both are activations of the same archetypal openness that has been elevated by grace. The anonymous Christian is present in the Buddhist because the same explicit archetypal movement toward Buddha is an implicit one toward Christ; they are both expressions of the same archetype. The Buddhist is an actual Buddhist because the archetype has been activated by the Buddha and an anonymous Christian because the activation by Christ is only potential. It is the same unconscious striving for wholeness that makes one an actual Buddhist and an anonymous Christian.

Conversely, an explicit archetypal movement toward Christ is an implicit one toward the Buddha. A Christian is an anonymous Buddhist. Rahner told Nishitani, the well-known Japanese philosopher and head of the Kyōto school, that he would be honored to be called an anonymous Zen Buddhist even though their understanding of its meaning might be different.

The archetypal approach allows one to understand the current academic discussion concerning the relationship between Christ and non-Christian religions. Raimundo Panikkar, professor emeritus at the University of California, Santa Barbara, has made a significant contribution to this discussion in his book, *The Unknown Christ of Hinduism* (1981). In commenting on the second and revised edition of this book theologian Joseph Wong writes that

> Christ is more than an historical figure [in Jesus]. As a universal principle Christ is the most powerful living symbol of the total reality which he calls "the Mystery." This symbol may assume other names, such as Rama, Krishna, or Isvara. Each name expresses the same Mystery, each dealing with an unknown dimension of Christ. . . . Thus Panikkar not only distinguishes between Jesus and Christ —, he actually separates the two when he affirms that the universal principle (Christ) is equally embodied in other religious figures. (Wong 1994, 618–19)

By contrast, Bede Griffiths, a scholar of East-West religious dialogue, claims that Christ as a living symbol and the historical Jesus should not be separate:

> While the idea of symbol is central to his reflection, Griffiths distinguishes between mythical symbol and

historic symbol. Rama and Krishna are mythical symbols belonging to the world of cyclic time with its endless recurrence (cf. Griffiths 1983, 125). By contrast
Jesus Christ is a symbol which is firmly "rooted in
history." Griffiths describes the Christ symbol as "an
event of supreme symbolism." Whereas Rama and
Krishna may have a universal meaning for human existence, the event of Jesus Christ is at once a symbolic
[archetypal] and historic event that has actually
changed human history by introducing a new consciousness and a new relationship with God (cf. 127–
28). (Wong 1994, 624–25)

Panikkar is treating Christ on the archetypal level
where all the great religious figures are actuations of the
same archetype. Griffiths is treating Christ on both the
archetypal and historical levels. On the archetypal level
Panikkar is correct. As an archetypal image, Christ is
a universal principle equally embodied in other religious
figures. On the historical level, however, with its differentiation from the archetype, for the believer Christ claims
uniqueness and is normative. But a question arises. Is the
acceptance of this claim necessary to accept Christ as an
archetypal image, as transhistorical?

For millions of Hindus apparently not. They remain
on the archetypal level, that of the transhistorical Christ.
On this level Christ truly transforms Hinduism without
being accepted historically. This recognition will take
time. Sister Kathleen Healy, who, according to Bede Griffiths, has produced an "extraordinarily comprehensive
study of the actual situation in India today," develops the

relationship between the archetypal, or transhistorical, and the historical presence of Christ in Hinduism.

> The Hindu does not seek the historic God-Man, the Jewish Messiah sent to redeem the world. But the Hindu is open to the transhistorical Christ who is the man Jesus and more than the man Jesus. The meeting point of Christian and Hindu is the everlasting resurrected Christ. There are not two Christs, however — the Christ who confronts the Hindu is the same Christ who confronts the Christian. Christ is both historical and transhistorical. He is the epiphany, the manifestation, of the Son of God in history, and he is also the mystery hidden from the beginning of time. The Hindu can understand the real Christ who was, is, and will be a living reality. This is the living Christ who can transform Hinduism through his incarnation, death, and resurrection. . . . Hinduism, like Christianity, awaits the radical transformation that will reveal more clearly the relationship of Jesus with the uncreated wisdom of the transhistorical Christ. (Healy 1990, 41)

It would seem that the implicit orientation in non-Christian religions toward Christ is one toward the transhistorical Christ and not the historical Jesus. Because on the archetypal level Buddha and Christ have the same value and are both transhistorical, there is no need to have an explicit knowledge of the historical Jesus. In other words, the historical life of Jesus remains on the level of myth, which has the function of expressing transhistorical truth. This is the reason why Rahner's claim that "the supernatural existential" therefore present in all humanity tends dynamically towards its irrevocable climax in Jesus Christ can be reconciled with the historical reality that there are billions of non-Christians who seem to have no desire for the historical Jesus. The orientation does not depend upon successful evangelization to accept the historical Jesus but on the fact that the transhistorical Christ is seen on the archetypal level as the exemplary cause of the entire history of salvation. Actually, it is the same Jesus, but not as the historical person who lived in a particular place and time but as the person who has a transhistorical archetypal meaning. The transhistorical image of Christ is what activates the archetype. Conversion consists in identifying the archetypal image with the historical Jesus. When this happens, the implicit presence of Christ becomes an explicit one. This answers Hans Kung, who finds difficulty in the fact that most Buddhist do not desire to become Christians, that is, to accept the historical Jesus (Kung 1976, 98).

To establish Christ as the end of creation Rahner uses a theology of the Incarnation. According to the Scotist school, "it is freely permitted to see the Incarnation first of all, in God's primary intention, as the summit and height of the divine plan of creation, and not primarily and in the first place as the act of a mere restoration of a divine world-order destroyed by the sins of mankind" (70). Secondly, Rahner develops a theology of the Resurrection. "In this beginning [the Resurrection] the destiny of the world is already in principle decided and has already begun. . . . [T]he risen Lord, freed by resurrection from the limiting individuality of the unglorified body" has a special relationship to the world (72–73). This theological position is confirmed both by Jung and Eliade. Jung uses depth psychology to show that Christ is the archetypal image or final cause of the individuation process. Eliade uses phenomenology to show that "pagan idolatry" is a prefiguration of the Incarnation, that is, it has an orientation toward Christ finding its fulfillment in Him. All three scholars agree that Christ is the final cause of human existence in the world.

Therefore, it is not only the universal religions, such as Hinduism and Buddhism, that activate the supernatural existential but also primal religions. Not only are they also part of the history of religions because primal religions do have a history but primarily Christ is also the final cause of creation. Christ is present in the cosmos as Word of God since the Logos becoming man "constitutes a hypostatic union with matter which attains to and commits itself to matter as such . . . [which is] why the total reality of the world is *ipso facto* touched to its very roots by the Incarnation of the Logos precisely in virtue of the fact that matter must be conceived of fundamentally and from the outset as one" (71). Rahner says that

> matter develops out of its inner being in the direction of the spirit. . . . Naturally, it would in itself be desirable to show more concretely what common traits are to be found in the evolution of material, living and spiritual beings — to show (more exactly) how the merely material is a prelude in its own dimensions to the higher

dimension of life, and how the latter in its dimension is
a prelude to the spirit in its ever greater advance towards the border line to be crossed by self transcendence. (65–67)

Jung does precisely this in stating that

> the position of the archetype would be located beyond
> the psychic sphere, analogous to the position of physio-
> logical instinct, which is immediately rooted in the stuff
> of the organism and, with its psychoid nature, forms
> the bridge to matter in general. . . . [The archetypes]
> are thus, essentially, the chthonic portion of the psyche
> . . . that portion through which the psyche is attached
> to nature, or in which its link with the earth and the
> world appears at its most tangible. (35–36)

The archetype rightly can be seen as the means through
which matter becomes spirit.

Christ is part of the entire evolutionary process beginning with matter self-transcending into spirit and continuing with the cosmos reaching consciousness in man and
with the self-bestowal of God reaching its climax in the
Incarnation as a unique manifestation of this self-
bestowal. Because of primal religion's close association
with nature, it becomes part of the mystery of the Incarnation because Christ incarnates the archetypal images of
nature in His unconscious as a part of His own humanity,
becoming part of the evolutionary process. This assumption of the archetypes is the psychological expression of

His cosmic presence as the Logos, Word of God, because the archetype is the link with the earth and the world as stated above.

Eliade also confirms the Incarnational aspect of the cosmic Christ. "From one point of view there has been no break in continuity from the 'primitives' to Christianity. The dialectic of the hierophany remains one, whether in an Australian churinga or in the Incarnation of the Logos. In both cases we are faced with a manifestation, vastly different obviously, of the sacred in a fragment of the universe" (9). Eliade shows that certain Fathers of the Church had a constant concern "to make manifest to unbelievers the correspondence between those great symbols which the soul finds immediately expressive and persuasive [the common property of humankind], and the dogmas of the new religion." Quoting Fr. Beirnaert, Eliade recognizes "a relationship between the dogmatic statements, the symbology of the Christian religion and the archetypes activated by the natural symbols" (19). Eliade's examples from the Fathers are amplifications of the Jungian archetypes and a confirmation of Rahner.

Finally, Rahner insists that the religious heritage of primal religion is what "Christianity and the Church must absorb and transform into themselves in order to become fully that which they already are" (58) or, in other words, to reach their full maturity. Christianity incorporates the values of primal religious symbolism, giving them a new meaning drawn from its own history, bringing together both archetypal and historical reality. According to Eliade, baptism instituted by Christ

in no way contradicts the universally diffused symbolism of water (17). . . . [The new Christian meaning]
does not radically modify the structure of the 'immanent' symbol (21). . . . Each new valorization of an archetypal Image crowns and consummates the earlier
ones —, the salvation revealed by the Cross does not
annul the prechristian values of the Tree of the World,
on the contrary, the Cross, that pre-eminent symbol of
the total renovatio, comes to complete all its earlier
valencies and meanings. (122–23)

The same can be said of the Sacred Pipe.

Observed from the point of view of Eliade's phenomenology, the archetypal symbols of primal religions are oriented toward Christ as a final goal. This orientation may
be unconscious, that is, the members of these primal religions may not necessarily know it. Eliade concludes, however, that "if at a certain moment in history a religious
symbol has been able to express clearly a transcendental
meaning [Rahner's supernatural existential] one is justified is supposing that this meaning might have been already grasped dimly at an earlier epoch" (27). This is the
same implicit knowledge that Rahner is talking about in
the anonymous Christian.

In summary, Eliade's phenomenology was seen as an
amplification of the Jungian archetypes. The claim was
made that Rahner's theology needed a psychology and a
phenomenology besides a philosophy as a foundation. The
archetypal movement toward wholeness, which produces
the archetype of the self, was identified with Rahner's

supernatural existential with its unlimited openness to the immediate presence of God. When elevated by grace, it becomes a new orientation to this presence by a new final goal manifested in a unique way in the Incarnation of Christ. Archetypal psychology was used to show how human spiritual nature was open to grace without demanding it and is not frustrated without it. The archetypal image charged with numinosity could be identified with the dynamism of the spirit because matter and spirit cannot be separated. Rahner's supernatural existential is also verified in Eliade's phenomenology in understanding symbols as opening humans to the universal, to the world of the spirit.

The archetypal approach clarifies the discussion on the relationship between Christ and non-Christian religions. Panikkar, in making Christ a universal principle equally embodied in other religious figures, is working on the archetypal level. Griffiths, however, maintains that Christ is not only a cyclic, or archetypal, symbol (so what Panikkar says is true) but also a historical person who claimed to be a unique expression of God's self-bestowal. For non-Christians to accept this uniqueness they must move from the archetypal to the historical level. This is facilitated by the historical Christ becoming an archetypal symbol that is not separated from His historical presence.

Primal religion activates the supernatural existential because Christ is the final goal not only of history but also of creation as Word of God and as Risen Christ. Christ was seen as part of the evolutionary process of matter self-transcending into spirit, of the cosmos becoming conscious in man. The archetype as a bridge between matter and spirit is the source of this self-transcendence into spirit. Primal religion becomes part of this Mystery of Christ because He assumed all the archetypes in His unconscious. These are the same archetypes that primal religion has activated to produce those natural religious symbols that the Fathers of the Church recognized as images of Christ through which He is attached to nature and the earth. Primal religions, then, are amplifications of the archetypes that are a part of Christ's humanity. There is a mutual fulfillment between Christ and non-Christian religions. Non-Christian religions find their fulfillment in Christ on an archetypal level, and Christ achieves His fulfillment in assuming non-Christian symbols as an extension of His Incarnation.

With these new insights I could now reread the ethnology of the Sacred Pipe among Native Americans with a new and more mature understanding and more correctly understand it as an archetypal image of Christ. I also was able to develop a model of religious identity that is a foundation for the Sacred Pipe as an image of Christ (1990, 176–93).

Some Lakota have separate beliefs in the traditional and Christian traditions, resulting in a split religious identity. This split, however, is healed by the recognition that they have common religious forms and are two expressions of the same sacred. I used the term, *Ecumenist* I for this position. At the time I thought that this recognition could achieve only limited stability (Steinmetz 1990, 192). I now think, however, that a very lasting stability can be achieved because both religious traditions involved are actuations of the same archetype with its numinosity as a source of power. This fact makes sincerity in dual participation in religious traditions not only possible but to be expected even in this position.

My observation is that many, if not most, of the medicine men and serious thinkers during the 1960s and 1970s went beyond recognizing the common religious forms in the two religious traditions and recognized their Lakota tradition as reaching a fulfillment in Christ because of the Christian faith that they had. I have presented evidence of this elsewhere (Steinmetz 1990, 189–91). I use the term *Ecumenist* II for this group's position. It is also important to recognize that the Ecumenist II position does not exclude the Ecumenist I position because the two religious traditions are still seen as expressions of the same sacred. In other words, the Ecumenist II position in going beyond the Ecumenist I still includes it.

My understanding of the Ecumenist II position, however, was not sufficiently nuanced. I came to realize that this position in which Lakota religion achieved its fulfillment in Christianity failed to recognize the mutual fulfillment that was necessarily concurrent in this position. Although the Sacred Pipe finds its fulfillment in Christ, Christ also finds His fulfillment in the Sacred Pipe. The former is true because the Sacred Pipe has an orientation to Christ as a Divine Incarnation that has a universal archetypal meaning for humankind and creation. The latter is true because the Incarnation is not complete until Christ assumes the religious traditions of humankind, in-

cluding that of the Sacred Pipe. Secondly, as the transhistorical Christ, He is an archetypal image truly present
in the Sacred Pipe and in His humanity. They both are
expressions, although not in the same way, of the same
sacred. And as the historical Jesus, He is unique, from
the point of view of faith, but not exclusive. Belief in
Christ does not exclude belief in the Sacred Pipe. Consequently, the Sacred Pipe has a validity in itself and does
not lose that validity even when it becomes a prefiguration
of Christ. It does not lose its archetypal value. And the
fact that there is the need for a mutual fulfillment under-
mines any notion of superiority. Although the Sacred Pipe
reaches its maturity in Christ as a prefiguration of Christ,
Christ reaches His maturity in the Sacred Pipe as a com-
pletion of His humanity. Consequently, the observation of
Clyde Holler, one of today's most perceptive scholars of
Native American religions, that "in any case it is clear that
for Steinmetz, the Lakota tradition is valid only insofar as
it is compatible with Christianity and accepts its fulfillment and perfection in it" is no longer valid (1995, 31).

William Powers, an anthropologist specializing in the
Lakota, rejects this model because of his misunder-
standing of dual participation. Holler summarizes his
position.

> Powers proposes that dual participation cannot be un-
> derstood if it is assumed that Christianity and native
> religion "fulfill the same needs rather than disparate
> ones," since this leads to the expectation that the two
> belief systems will collide and produce "either tension

or conflation" (Powers 1987, 100). The solution is to discard the assumption that we are dealing with bireligion or "dual religious belief," since participation is different from belief: "I agree that indeed he cannot believe in two religions, but this is not to say that he cannot participate in more than one" (100). If Christianity and traditional religion both functioned as belief systems, the expectation would be that they would be syncretized. Among the Oglala, however, they coexist rather than conflate, which can only be understood on the basis of a structural-functional model: "I will argue that Christianity and Oglala religion coexist because they serve quite disparate functions" (102). In effect, while traditional religion meets religious needs, Christianity meets social and economic needs. (Holler 1995, 205–6)

Powers's argument is flawed for several reasons. First, Christianity and Oglala religion do not simply coexist. They are both seen as manifestations of the sacred, the Ecumenist I position, which already is more than coexistence. And for some medicine men and more serious thinkers this developed into a vision of the mutual fulfillment of both religious traditions, the Ecumenist II position.

Second, Powers suffers from the limitations of social anthropology with its structural-functional model. Studying only the social functions of religion leads Powers to the false conclusion that people can belong to two religious traditions only if they fulfill disparate needs. Understanding the social functions of religion can never be the

means of understanding its essential nature. Rather, a phenomenological model, such as Eliade's (1958, 1–33),
shows that despite all the diversity one finds the structure
of religious experience is the same, giving another verification that dual religious belief is possible and even to be
expected.

Third, Powers's claim that the two religious traditions
cannot fulfill the same needs but only disparate ones leads
him to the assumption that Lakota religion meets religious
needs and Christianity meets social and economic needs.
This is obviously false to anyone who has done pastoral
ministry on the Pine Ridge Reservation. From my own
personal experience Ben Black Elk, son of the famous
Black Elk, could not have been any more sincere in seeking purification in a sweat lodge ceremony than he was in
receiving the Catholic Sacrament of Reconciliation. And
the medicine man George Plenty Wolf walked one mile to
and one mile back from church on Sunday when he was
half-blind. When medicine man Frank Fools Crow became sick during the 1980 tribal Sun Dance and retired
to his tent, he asked me to give him the Sacrament of the
Anointing of the Sick and Holy Communion on the Sun
Dance grounds. He did not ask for one of the Lakota
medicine men to pray over him. They, and many other
Lakota, were fulfilling religious needs and not social or
economic ones. Powers's false assumption simply does not
stand up to the facts. He loses all sense of objectivity in
tending to interpret the Catholic priests praying with the
Sacred Pipe "as a strategy designed to win converts
through a kind of moral deception, one deemed acceptable

because the stratagem would ultimately lead to a civilized revelation rather than a primitive vision" (1987, 99). He is simply being judgmental and making an unsubstantiated accusation.

Actually, both religious traditions meet all the needs of the people: religious, social, and economic. *Yuwipi* meetings (in which petitions are made through the spirits) fulfill social needs for the community and economic support for the medicine man as well as spiritual needs. The Christian churches not only fulfilled social and economic needs but also religious ones.

Fourth, there is no need for tension between the two traditions because Lakota religion is an extension of Christ's Humanity as Rahner proposed in his theological development. Any claim about the uniqueness of Christ in Lakota religion is not exclusive, that is, it recognizes the latter's validity. On the Pine Ridge Reservation, however, tensions sometimes did exist. To cite but one example, Ben Black Elk lived with tension. He told me that "through most of his life there was a conflict between these two traditions. He did have doubts of conscience. When he lectured on the Sacred Pipe and had a belief in the Sacred Pipe, was he betraying himself as a Christian? He said that now that he sees that the Sacred Pipe and Christ really are one, that they fulfill each other, the doubts of conscience of many years have ended" (Steinmetz 1990, 203). Ben Black Elk also had an understanding of mutual fulfillment.

My journey also helped me arrive at a theological explanation of the essential attitudes of primal religions, in-

cluding Native Americans ones. The first is a oneness with
creation with its lack of clear distinction between human
and nature. Rahner says that

> the one material cosmos is, as it were, the one body of
> the *multifarious* self-presence of this self-same cosmos
> [in humans]. . . . For in his corporeality, every man is
> an element of the cosmos which cannot really be de-
> limited and cut off from it, and in this corporeality, he
> communicates with the whole cosmos in such a way
> that through this corporeality of man taken as the other
> element of belonging to the spirit, the cosmos really
> presses forward to this self-presence in the spirit. (67)

Another essential attitude in Native American religions is the presence of spirits in the entire world of nature. This belief is confirmed by Rahner's development of
the nature of angels. He says that because angels "reach
down to or into the material world, these functions must
ultimately be based on the nature of the angels — the
angels can be understood quite correctly, even according
to scripture, as cosmic (even though personal) powers of
the order of nature and its history. . . . They are powers of
the one and hence also material world to whose material
nature they are genuinely and essentially related" (68).
Thus, according to Rahner, the spirits that Native Americans believe to be present in nature can be seen as the
same as the angels of Christianity.

A third essential attitude is the sense of sacramentalism. Rahner states that the historian of religions must

"discover in a concrete and religious form those 'sacraments of nature' which the dogmatic theologian postulates in the abstract" (64). Eliade reminds the reader that "certain Fathers of the Church have examined the interesting correspondence between the archetypal images evoked by Christianity and the images which are the common property of mankind" (18). The Sacred Pipe and its ceremonies are these "sacraments of nature" and are the images "which are the common property of mankind." These "Images provide 'openings' into a transhistorical world." It opens one to the universal religious experience of humankind, which, although expressed through historical events, is a transcendental experience beyond history. The Sacred Pipe with all its ceremonies taking place in history is also a religious symbol that takes one into the mystery of the cosmic Christ present in the whole world of creation. The Sacred Pipe activates the supernatural existential with its unlimited openness to God that has been orientated to Christ as a final goal.

5

The Ethnology of the Sacred Pipe

One needs more than to understand the Sacred Pipe as
an archetypal image of Christ in the abstract. One needs
to explore its ethnology. The Sacred Pipe in American
Indian religions has a unique position in the history of
primal religions throughout the world in the wide variety
of symbolism associated with it and in its many ceremonial
uses. My purpose here is to bring together an abundance
of ethnographic data so that the religious meaning of the
Sacred Pipe can be understood and appreciated and can
later be seen as an appropriate archetypal image of Christ.
I present the Sacred Pipe for its own sake and not simply
in its social functions. The Sacred Pipe's ultimate meaning
is in its sacramental nature because it is a Native American symbol that makes all of life sacred.

An Overview

There were many different kinds of pipes. Although
they were common to all tribes, their religious meanings

and sacramental uses were very diverse, and there were nonsacramental uses of the pipe as well. Although the first pipes were made from the bones of animals and are undoubtedly the oldest (Hodge 1910, 2:257; Wallace and Hoebel 1952, 98), elaborately carved effigy pipes, which are equal to the best productions of Mexico and Peru, have been discovered in the mounds of the Mississippi Valley and are at least one thousand years old (Squier and Davis 1848, 246, viii). It appears that simple tubular pipes were characteristic of the entire United States and Central America, but other types were more localized. The well-known catlinite pipe bowl dates only from the beginning of the nineteenth century (Wedel 1961, 123). This pipe is called catlinite because George Catlin sent a sample of the pipe stone to Boston for analysis (Catlin 1841, 2:206). The Catlin manuscript in the British Museum is a valuable document that contains drawings by the author (Catlin 1979). Material in the U.S. National Museum is also important for its numerous examples of many kinds of pipes (McGuire 1899). George West classifies nineteen different types of pipes and gives their locations throughout North America in a series of maps. Volume 1 contains the text and volume 2 an excellent collection of photographs (1934). Jordan Paper presents the ritual, mythology, symbolism, geography, history and recent revitalization of the Sacred Pipe in an excellent introduction (1988). John Ewers published an important study after examining almost two thousand effigy carvings and extensive literature of early travelers (1986). He analyzes animal effigy bowls, including the bear, beaver, bighorn sheep, buffalo, dog, horse, bird, snake, fish, and combinations of these animals (52–82). Among the bowls depicting people he develops four themes:

1. Attitude toward the white man considered as possessing supernatural power because of his weapons and tools of iron. One pipe bowl representing an Indian and white man looking each other in the face, however, was interpreted by the Native American carver as an Indian "not afraid to look the white man in the face."

2. Iktomi, the Sioux trickster, "a mischievous little imp who repeatedly and ridiculously got into trouble with the other creatures of this world."

3. Attitude toward the liquor trade, including possession as an honorable achievement.

4. Attitude toward women depicted as sex objects, including one that is the "frank portrayal of a man and woman making love." These pipes may have been especially carved to amuse white friends (92–104).

Excellent photographs accompany the text.

Trade among tribes was a major means of the wide distribution of the Sacred Pipe. Native Americans apparently carried pipes as far as one thousand miles for trade. In 1892 it was claimed that not even 1 percent of the pipes were manufactured by Native Americans. They sold much of the pipe stone to White traders, who produced pipes on lathes near the quarry at Pipestone, Minnesota. Between 1860 and 1866 the Northeastern Fur Company manufactured nearly two thousand pipes and traded them with the Native Americans of the upper Missouri (Holmes 1919, 262–63).

There were however, considerable differences in the use of the Sacred Pipe by the Native American tribes. Among the California tribes the religious offering of tobacco and the smoking of pipes were limited in practice (Kroeber 1925, 826). During the Yurok Jump Dance, a salmon rite held by the river at Wetlkwau, the individual in charge of the ceremony kept a pipe that was regarded with the greatest fear (60). A Yokut shaman could both cause and cure sickness by blowing pipe smoke over the patient. Although most pipes were made of pottery, shamans used ancient stone pipes (653). Pipes were generally small and crudely made because the common practice of all the tribes was to eat tobacco instead of smoking it. Ingested tobacco served as an emetic and was thought to impart supernatural efficacy (538). Among the Luiseno Tribe the first step in the puberty ceremony was to make the girls swallow balls of tobacco as an ordeal. Only those who did not vomit were considered virtuous (674).

In the Pueblo area of the Southwest simple tubes were almost universal except for the elbow pipes developed in recent years (Fewkes 1895–96, 734). Henry Schoolcraft states that a pipe of serpentine rock, a straight tube that admits a wooden handle, was used in Navajo ceremonies (1856, 4:435–36). J. Walter Fewkes states that smoking a huge stemless pipe was one of the most sacred acts performed by the Antelope priest during the Tusayan Snake Dance at Walpi in Hopi. The priest "blew several dense clouds of smoke upon the sand altar so that the picture was concealed" (Fewkes 1895–96, 734). The smoke was considered emblematic of rain clouds and, thus, the term *cloud blower* was used as a description of the pipe (Roberts 1931, 149). The tobacco pouch was a ceremonial property often depicted in sand paintings as a possession of Sun and Moon (Reichard 1970, 605).

An entirely different use of the pipe is found in Alaska where the Eskimo felt an Asian influence from Siberia and used smoking as a means of intoxication (Harrington 1932, 183; Murdoch 1887–88, 70–71). In the eastern part of the United States the pipe was known as the Calumet or Peace Pipe, becoming a major symbol of the Native American (Fenton 1953, 152–206; West 1934, 1: 231–48). Among the Plains and Prairie tribes the pipe achieved a unique importance. Luis Kemnitzer states that "if any one artifact symbolized the identity, history and religion of the Lakota . . . it is the pipe" (1970, 44). I found among the Lakota that no religious ceremony ever takes place without it. The same is true of the Montana Cree (Dusenberry 1962, 117).

Although the pipe is frequently called a Peace Pipe, there is also a War Pipe used to organize and lead war parties. A Tomahawk Pipe was also used both in connection with peace and war (McGee 1893–94, 172). Most pipes were smoked by one person at a time. James Mooney, however, states that the Cherokee had a pipe bowl with seven holes to be smoked at peace councils by seven people at the same time (1897–98, 397).

Pipes were also in constant use for nonsacramental purposes, including for pleasure, a fact established by early travelers. In 1637 the Jesuit Fathers noticed that the Native Americans in the Quebec area were excessive smokers and that a missionary should provide himself with a tinderbox or a burning mirror to light their pipes (Thwaites 1896–1901, 12:117). Steven R. Riggs states that smoking takes up much of their time. When the camp moves, the women pack and start off while the men sit down and take a last smoke (1869, 21–22). Catlin claims that there was no custom more uniformly constant in use nor higher in value (1841, 1:235). When this developed is uncertain. Clark Wissler says that the Native Americans apparently smoked for pleasure where tobacco was plentiful. In areas where it was less abundant it was saved for ceremonial purposes (Wissler 1966, 65). But, according to George A. West "smoking for pleasure seems to have developed among the Indians after the advent of the white man" (West 1934, 1:238).

Although Gladys Nomland gives an example of a northern California Athabascan woman shaman who smoked an old tubular pipe (1931), apparently it was not the general practice for women to smoke in precontact days, but in trade days the older women were fond of smoking for pleasure, using a smaller pipe than that preferred by the men (Wissler 1966, 65). Perhaps, one could argue as Jordan Paper does that it was a normal practice for women to pray with the Sacred Pipe in religious ceremonies because a male ethnologist would have ignored female leaders and would not have been invited to female societies (1988, 38). The absence of sufficient positive evidence for this assertion, however, makes the extent of female use a matter of speculation.

The Sacred Pipe in Mythology

Mythology is the primary source of the Sacred Pipe's sacramental nature. "The pipe holds an important part in the mythology and ritual of almost all our tribes, east and west" (Mooney 1892–93, 14:1063). The pipe is used even in the passing on of myths. The Arapaho and the Gros Ventre recite the origin of the land and the manner in which the pipe and the corn were given to the ancestors during the ceremony of uncovering the pipe, but the Arapaho refuse to tell the myth in its entirety so that only fragments of it have been recorded by the white man (Carter 1938, 73). The corresponding Cheyenne myth takes four smokes, that is, four consecutive nights to relate. "So sacred is this tradition held that no one but the priest of the pipe dares to recite it, for fear of divine punishment should the slightest error be made in the narration" (Mooney 1892–93, 14:960). Among the Kiowas "come and smoke invitations" were shouted by the host in front of his tipi where the pipe was passed around and smoked while men recounted the tribal myths (Mayhall 1962, 16).

Myths give a unique meaning to the pipes of various tribes. To see how true this is I examine

1. Creation myths
2. Myths relating the Sacred Pipe to nature
3. Variations of the Lakota myth of the Woman bringing the Calf Pipe
4. Myths relating the Sacred Pipe to the pipe stone

5. Myths relating the Sacred Pipe to magic
6. Myths of the origin of tobacco.

Creation Myths

In creation mythology the Sacred Pipe is associated with Sacred Time, the time in the beginning, the "illo tempore" of Mircea Eliade. The Sacred Pipe is sacramental because it makes Sacred Time present now. In a Gros Ventre myth the primeval keeper of the Flat Pipe, known as Earthmaker, was the only human to survive a flood. He made a raft of logs and put the pipe on it. He sent animal survivors to the bottom of the waters to bring up the mud from which the earth was made. Because he was the only human survivor, he was lonely and so made a man and a woman from the mud. He taught them about the pipe and, when the people multiplied, they followed its teaching (Cooper 1957, 435–37). In an Arapaho version Earthmaker was floating in a pipe bowl instead of the raft (435). In a Hidatsa myth First Creator and Lone Man were co-makers of the earth. First Creator caused the people who were living below to come up, bringing with them their garden produce. The people came up, following a vine until one woman heavy in pregnancy broke the vine. Lone Man carried a wooden pipe, but he did not know what it was used for. First Creator ordered Male Buffalo to produce tobacco for Lone Man's pipe. This act explains the use of pipes in religious rituals and the concept of tobacco as something sacred (Bowers 1965, 298). In a

Caddo myth men and animals were brothers living under the ground. When they discovered the entrance of the cave leading up to the earth's surface, an old man was the first to climb up, carrying in one hand fire and a pipe and in the other a drum. His wife came up next with corn and pumpkin seeds. As soon as the wolf came up, he closed up the hole so that some of the people and animals remained below. Because they had the pipe, drum, corn and pumpkin seed, they were a People (Mooney 1892–93, 14:1093–94). In a Montana Cree myth before the Creator went far away where no one would see him, he left four important things: "Fire, Pipe (and the rock from which the pipe is made), Pipe stem (and the tree from which the stem is made), and sweet grass. The tobacco is already in the pipe." He told them that these are the things to use to make any connection with Him (Dusenberry 1962, 66).

Myths Relating the Sacred Pipe to Nature

Myths relating the Sacred Pipe to nature make it a sacramental expression of one of the basic Native American values, that of being in harmony with nature. All of nature is included from a tiny worm to the stars and the thunder as is shown in the following Blackfoot myths. A hunter was sitting in bed smoking before a large decayed piece of burning wood. He saw a worm crawling along it and heard singing. The worm became a person holding a medicine pipe with a straight tubular bowl and a decorated stem. While singing "the fire is my medicine," the worm person transferred the pipe to the man. In the second myth a hunter came to a mountaintop to fast for four days. He heard singing from above: "The Seven Stars say, 'My pipe is powerful.' Old Man says, 'My pipe is powerful. He hears me'.'" The smallest star became a person and gave him a medicine pipe. In another myth after a hunter killed four elk, he heard Coyote singing: "Fine meat, I want to eat it." The hunter gave an elk to Coyote in return for a medicine pipe. In a final myth a girl married Thunder and was taken to a high mountain lodge. An old man taught his daughter-in-law how to bring in the bundle containing the medicine pipe. She gave birth to two boys. The Thunder allowed her to return to her parents' lodge to announce that she would return in four days to bring the medicine pipe. Thunder came with the woman, the two boys, and the pipe. After the ceremony of transferring the pipe took place, Thunder left the younger child. Now, when Thunder threatens, the people say that for the sake of the younger child he heeds their prayers (Wissler 1908, 89–91).

In Wichita mythology a star named "I am a Young Man When the Dawn Comes Up" gave a black pipe and a white eagle feather to a young man at dawn. He took the pipe in a gesture of blessing and carefully blessed himself with the feather. The star instructed the young man to speak to him in a beseeching way at dawn so that he could take pity on him (Curtis 1907–30, 19:88–89). In another myth a young man walked over the water to where a beautiful woman with a black pipe was standing. She told him to ask for whatever he desired. He made the mistake of desiring her beauty. On admitting his guilt, however, he chose the black pipe. She instructed him that before hunting he should throw the first puff of smoke to the water for that is hers and he would have plenty of food. The name of the spirit was "Woman Forever in the Water." (19:94). In Seneca mythology the husband of the chief's youngest daughter lit and smoked his pipe. "The bull frog [carved on the bowl] croaked and the black snake [carved on the stem] tried to swallow the bull frog. All the people looked on in wonder, and they said, 'We have never before seen a man with orenda so powerful' " (Curtin and Howitt 1910–11, 134).

Variations of the Lakota Myth of the Women Bringing the Calf Pipe

In a famous Lakota myth a woman brings the Calf Pipe. Its many versions dramatize how different meanings are associated with the Sacred Pipe even within the same tribal tradition. For example, the Black Elk version, as related to Joseph Brown, gives the ceremonial meaning, whereas in the Philip Perch version it is associated with war. In fact, each version of the Lakota tradition has its own unique contribution to the sacramental nature of the Sacred Pipe. In a time of famine two hunters looking for buffalo saw a beautiful woman coming from the sky. One hunter had evil desires toward her and was reduced to a skeleton. The woman instructed the other hunter to prepare the people for her return. Preparations were made, and the people were all excited. Suddenly, she appeared, entered the lodge, and presented the pipe. She told them that their prayers through the pipe would always be answered. As she left, she turned into a buffalo calf from which the pipe receives its name.

This is the basic myth. Eleven versions, however, are the source of widely different meanings of the Calf Pipe. In the Black Elk versions, as recorded by Joseph Brown in 1948, the pipe became the center of seven religious ceremonies: Sweat Lodge, Vision Quest, Girls' Puberty Rite, Keeping the Soul, Making Relatives, the Sun Dance, and Throwing the Ball. A red stone with seven circles symbolized these rites (Brown 1953, 3–9). Black Elk gave a much briefer account to John Neihardt in 1932, mentioning only one ceremony, the Keeping of the Soul, but instead giving an incident not found in Brown:

> Some hunters went out and got a buffalo and it was in the spring of the year when the calves are in the womb yet. They got the insides out and found a calf in it and cut the womb open and to their surprise it was a human in there. It looked like an old woman. The hair was pure white. All the men gathered there and saw it. This actually happened 80 years ago. (DeMallie 1984, 285)

The difference between these two accounts is so great that it is likely that the Black Elk account in Brown was the result of Black Elk's reflection between 1932 and 1948, which proves how living and developing a mythological tradition is.

Nevertheless, there are other versions of the basic myth; I summarize only the important differences. According to the Finger versions, the woman was "without clothing of any kind except that her hair was very long and fell over her body like a robe." The woman told the good hunter that when she entered the village, "the men must all sit with their heads bowed and look at the ground until she was in their midst." One man failed to do this, and a puff of black smoke blew into his eyes so that from then on he had very sore eyes as if biting smoke was in them. The woman entered the circle and served food first to the little children and then to the women and then she bade the men to look up and served them (Walker 1980, 109–11). Thomas Tyon confirms that the woman was very beautiful and completely naked with long hair (149). A contemporary Lakota medicine man told me that she was completely naked as a temptation to the hunters.

In the Sword version the woman feigned to give the pipe three times and gave it the fourth time, a ceremonial practice still in use today. She stayed four days and taught them everything possible. She told them that buffalo and other animals were to be eaten but that certain foods were forbidden: snake, lizards, toads, crabs, buzzard, eagle, owl, crow, hawk, magpie, cat, moles, weasels, and squirrels. She also said that those who fought within the tribe must be friends. But those who were enemies (outside the tribe) were not to be friends, and as enemy outsiders will remain. She said that everything done in warfare was to be accounted as good deeds. The chiefs were to use the pipe to resolve a feud that would develop from avenging a murder within the tribe (Deloria 1938, 21–23).

Percy Phillips states that from the first enemy that shall be killed through the power of the pipe an ear shall be cut off and tied to the pipe-stem. The first scalp to be taken shall be treated in the same way. . . . A few days after the pipe had been brought, there was a quarrel within the camp in which two people were killed. In accordance with the woman's command they cut the ear from one and tied it to the pipe stem, together with the scalp, and that ear and scalp are on the pipe to this day. (G. Dorsey 1906, 327–28)

Ernest Two Runs said that "after the woman left, they went buffalo hunting and found the woman among the buffalo; so they killed the woman and cut off her ears and tied them to the Calf Pipe, now meaning 'Whatever I hear with my ears is the meaning of my generation' " (Meekel n.d., 3).

John Smith reports:

From the quiver on her back she took six bows and arrows. These she gave to six young men known for their bravery and truthfulness. She told these men to go to the top of a certain hill where there grazed six hundred buffalo. In the middle of this herd would be found six men. These men were to be killed and their ears cut off and attached to the stem of the Sacred Calf Pipe. (J. Smith 1967, 3)

In the Lone Man version speeches are prominent. The chief makes a speech welcoming the maiden, and she in turn gives lengthy speeches concerning daily living to the whole tribe and individually to the women, children, the men, and, finally, to the chief. She said that "the time will come when you shall cease hostilities against other nations. Whenever peace is agreed upon between two tribes or parties this pipe shall be a binding instrument" (Densmore 1918, 65–66).

In the Iron Shell version the woman represents the Buffalo People and is proud to be a sister to the Lakota. She talked four days with the women, children, men, and the leader on how to take care of the pipe. Before leaving, she lit the pipe and offered it to the Sky, the Earth, and the Four Directions (Hassrick 1964, 257–60).

In an account of Captain J. M. Lee one hunter was about to kill the woman because she was not of their own tribe. She said that the purpose of the pipe was to establish peace within the tribe and no one who kills a member of his own tribe must be allowed to smoke it (Mooney 1892–93 14:1062–63).

Finally, Garrick Mallery gives another version in his explanation of the Baptiste Good winter count:

> With the pipe she gave them a small package, in which they found four grains of maize, one white, one black, one yellow and one variegated. The pipe is above the buffalo. She said, "I am a buffalo, the White Buffalo Cow. I will spill my milk over the earth, that the people may live." She meant by her milk maize, which is seen in the picture dropping from her udders. (Mallery 1888–89, 290)

Myths Relating the Sacred Pipe to the Pipe Stone

In another important Sioux myth the Great Spirit called the American Indian nations to Pipestone Quarry, stood on the precipice of the red pipe stone rock, broke off a piece and made a huge pipe, smoking it in the Four Directions. He told them that the stone was red because it was their flesh and that they must use it for pipes of peace and avoid war on this land. At the last puff of the pipe his head went into a great cloud and the whole surface of the rock was melted and glazed for several miles (Catlin 1841, 2:164). When Catlin was 150 miles away from the quarry, he was surrounded by a group of angry, threatening Sioux who told him that "as this red stone was a part of their flesh, it would be sacrilegious for the white man to touch or take it away . . . because a hole would be made in their flesh and the blood could never be made to stop running" (166). But, as was shown above, a few years later the Native Americans were selling it to the White man, showing how quickly religious attitudes change. The quarry was visited for centuries by many tribes" who have hidden the war club as they approached it, and stayed the cruelties of the scalping knife, under fear of the vengeance of the Great Spirit, who overlooks it" (166–67). At a later date, however, a Mandan complained to Catlin that the Sioux had taken over the quarry for their own use exclusively. "My friend, we want to visit our medicine — our pipes are old and worn out. My friend, I wish you to speak to our Great Father [in Washington, D.C.] about this" (170).

According to Beckwith, the red pipe stone was the blood of two rival American Indian tribes who were at war with each other, and the pipe was given to achieve peace. Among the Arikara the red stone is the blood of the original buffalo "whose horns seem to reach the sky (Beckwith 1930, 425). A contemporary Lakota told me that "the red pipe bowl is the Indian's blood, the blood of a woman. The stem is the breath of a man. The two together guarantee the future generations. If the pipe is lost, it will be the end of the Sioux people" (Looking Horse 1979).

Myths Relating the Sacred Pipe to Magic

In Navajo mythology the Sacred Pipe is associated with magical practices. This reflects the Navajos' preoccupation with witchcraft, which is present among the Plains tribes only to a minimal degree. In one myth two boys went on a journey to see their father, the Sun. The Sun tested them to see if they were his sons. As one of the tests the Sun offered them four large pipes to smoke. The wind warned them that the tobacco was poisonous, but they smoked and remained unharmed. After passing all the tests, a rainbow bridge was placed across the water so that they could pass on (Curtis 1907–30, 1:102–4). The San Carlos Apache have a similar myth in which the spider spins a thread from one boy to the house of the Black Sun for him to travel on (Goddard 1918, 9–11).

Another Navajo myth relates the pipe to the Night Chant ceremony. Two jeweled pipes lay beside a god sitting on the western side of the hogan. He filled the pipes with tobacco, lit them, and passed one each to his right and his left, and all assembled smoked. Two large owls, one on each side of the entrance, were the last to smoke. They drew in deep drafts and puffed them out violently and countless people came in from all directions. At midnight lightning flashed, followed by heavy thunder and rain that Water Sprinkler sent in anger because he had not been informed of the dance before it began. But a smoke with the assembled Holy People appeased him. Soon after the chant began and continued until morning (Curtis 1907–30, 1:115).

In a final Navajo myth Frog, a mythical being with magical powers, had a turquoise pipe that he filled with tobacco and lighted by holding it to the Sun. He inhaled the smoke, and it came out of the holes all over his body. Rainboy was warned not to smoke the pipe nor to pick up a magic stone axe because both actions would kill him (Reichard 1970, 439–40).

I found only one myth relating the pipe to magic outside the Navajo tradition. The strongest living Mandan man, who defeated White people in several wrestling matches,

> always takes hold of his pipe by the head, for were he to touch another part of it the blood would suddenly rush from his nostrils. As soon as he bleeds in this manner he empties his pipe, throwing the contents into the fire, where it explodes like gunpowder, and the

bleeding stops immediately. They said nobody can
touch this man's face without bleeding at nose and
mouth. (J. Dorsey, 1889–90, 511)

Myths of the Origin of Tobacco

Several myths relate to the origin of tobacco. Because
the Sacred Pipe is never used in ceremony without tobacco, these myths are important in understanding its
meaning. The fact that tobacco must be stolen from the
gods brings out its superhuman nature.

In an Iroquois myth a boat filled with medicine men
passed near a village, causing death to some of the inhabitants. The next day those who escaped death found strange
beings asleep at each end of the boat. A loud voice told
them that they would receive a great blessing by destroying these creatures. So the villagers burned them and from
their ashes rose the tobacco plant (E. Smith 1880–81, 79).

According to a Menominee myth, a man detected a
delightful odor, which he discovered was tobacco. A giant
guarding it told him that he would have to wait one year
because the spirits had just smoked during their annual
ceremony. The man, however, stole a pouch of tobacco
and was pursued by the giant. When the man "reached a
certain prominent peak, the opposite side of which was a
high cliff, he suddenly lay flat on the rocks while the giant
leaped over him and down into the chasm beyond." The
man was then able to throw the bruised giant violently to
the ground. He told him that for his meanness he would

become a grasshopper, "the jumper," a pest to those who raise tobacco (Hoffman 1892–93, 14:205–6).

In a Cherokee myth an old man had to be kept alive by smoking and, as a consequence, the tobacco was used up. The son took a hummingbird skin out of his medicine bag, put it on, and turned into a hummingbird. He flew over the mountains to the tobacco field and put some of the leaves and seed into his medicine bag. He was so small and swift the guards did not notice him. On his return he took off the hummingbird skin and turned back into a man again. "He found his father very weak, but still alive and one draw at the pipe made him strong again. The people planted the seed and have had tobacco since" (Lowie 1920, 112). It was an elaborate ceremony (161–73) with a mythological tradition (176–89).

Native American Attitudes
Toward the Sacred Pipe

Native American attitudes toward the Sacred Pipe further understanding of its sacramental nature by showing that the pipe is set apart and, consequently, is surrounded by taboos and strict rules. Its power must be safeguarded. Because the Sacred Pipe is both beneficial and dangerous, it is both loved and feared. This is especially true of a tribe's original pipe. These attitudes help one to appreciate the ambivalence of the sacred.

To the American Indians Pipestone Quarry in Minnesota was a sacred place that demanded respect and special taboos as documented by Sidney Ball:

L. N. Nicollet, who visited the quarry . . . in 1838–39
(1843, 15–17), adds that the Indians believe that when
they visit the quarry, they are always saluted by lightning and thunder and that its discovery was due to a
deep path worn down into the catlinite bed by the buffalo. . . . Three days of purification preceded the Indians' visit to the quarry during which time he who was
to do the quarrying must be continent. The Abbé Domenech (1860, 2:347) adds that during this period the
miners fasted. Provided the pit, which the Indian miner
sinks, does not encounter catlinite of good quality, he is
considered to have "impudently boasted of his purity.
He is compelled to retire; and another takes his place."
A Sioux who visited the quarry about that time says
that first there was a feast to the spirits of the place
and then before quarrying a religious dance was held
(Dodge 1877, XLVII). The Indians (Domenech 1860,
2:273) were loath to have white men visit the quarry
as their presence was a profanation which would
draw down the wrath of heaven on the Indians. (Ball
1941, 49)

Respect for the Sacred Pipe was expressed in the observance of sexual taboos.

The Lakota had a great fear of the morning after sexual
intercourse, especially those who are official pipe carri-
ers or lance bearers or who hold any office [in the
akicita societies]. They fear to smoke a pipe because it
may blind them or hurt them otherwise. In the summer
they bathe in the creek to cleanse themselves and thus

be at liberty to smoke, and in the winter they wash their privates. (Walker 1982, 96)

Even today a woman in her menstrual period should not be in the presence of the pipe during a ceremony. In Pete Catches's mind this taboo does not involve impurity but a feminine power resulting from her special relationship to nature at this time, which neutralizes the power of the medicine man. He claimed that a woman failed to do this one time and that her bleeding never stopped and she died.

The Sacred Pipe was closely associated with fire. Schoolcraft states that American Indians used a sacred fire "extracted from its latent form in the flint. . . . It is the duty of a particular official to attend to this rite . . . to employ ordinary fire from embers, would appear to have the effect, in their minds, of employing strange fire" (1856, 5:65). According to Thomas Nuttall, the great rite of religion throughout North America was the pipe; "associated with this adoration . . . was that of preserving an eternal fire in some sacred place appropriated for this purpose" (Thwaites 1904–7, 13:346). This observance was also important for the Sioux:

> On marches, coals from the previous council fire were carefully preserved and used to rekindle the council fire at the new campsite. The council fire itself was the symbol of the group's autonomy . . . coals from which were used to light the pipe. . . . Sharing of a common fire may be seen as one of the integrating symbols of Sioux society. (Walker 1982, 12)

Among the Omaha the Tribal Pipes were not easily displayed to the tribe as a source of unity. Consequently, a cedar pole was selected to take the place of the pipes. At the consecration of the Sacred Pole the pipe belonging to it was ceremonially smoked. The act of smoking was a prayer of consecration that asked for a blessing on the anointing about to take place. The pole was anointed with a mixture of buffalo fat, the symbol of abundance, and red paint, the symbol of life, which together symbolized an abundant life (Fletcher and LaFlesche 1905–6, 1:217). If a mistake occurred during the ceremonies,

> the ones who had charge of the Sacred Pole and its rites, arose, lifted their arms, held their hands with palms upward, and standing thus in the attitude of supplication, wept. After a few moments one of the official servers came forward, passed in front of the line of standing singers and wiped the tears from each man's face . . . and the ceremony began again from the beginning as though for the first time. (232)

The Cheyenne had strict rules for praying with the pipe. No one was allowed to enter or leave the lodge, to scatter the ashes, to make sudden noises, or to walk between the smoker and the fire (Grinnell 1972, 1:74–75). The Arapaho believed that handling the pipe incorrectly caused rain when it was undesired (Hilger 1952, 94). One woman told Sr. Inez Hilgard, "I don't like to talk about the pipe. Only people who handle the pipe should talk about it" (159). At the installation of a chief among the

Omaha a man whose duty it was to fill the pipe let one of them fall to the ground, violating a law and preventing the continuation of the ceremony. He died shortly after. When the Otoes visited the Omaha in the summer of 1878 certain pipes were uncovered without the prescribed prayers. The keeper of the Pipes soon died, followed by his daughter and eldest son (J. Dorsey 1881–82, 224).

The Cheyenne chief, Little Wolf, while drunk, killed Standing Elk in a fit of anger: "Immediately after the killing Little Wolf smashed his long stemmed pipe, the symbol of the Chief's office. He was permitted to smoke one of the short pipes made from the leg bone of a deer, but he denied himself even this. Smoking was basically sacred work, so he never smoked again" (Powell 1969, 2:290–91).

When a Crow spared his life, the head of a Lakota family spared the life of another Crow enemy in return by putting him into the tipi containing the Sacred Pipe (Curtis 1907–30, 4:103). During a long battle the Assinboine shot and killed the Blood Pipe bearer and seized the medicine pipe. There were so many Blood Indians around the victim that the Assinboine could not count coup. The Assinboine were in a desperate position without ammunition. The Blood women told them that if they returned the pipe, they would cease fighting and they would be saved. Then the man who shot the Blood Indian approached; all laid down their guns and raised their arms in gratitude. They spread the finest blankets and he laid the pipe on them. The dead man's relatives filled the pipe and made the Assinboine smoke it. They heaped up blankets, moccasins, armlets, and even an abundant supply of ammunition in return for the pipe (Lowie 1909, 51).

Faith in the power of the pipe was deep. The Cheyenne say that the pipe never fails (Powell 1969, 1:14). According to a Blackfoot story, when the people were unable to cross a high river, Weasel Heart parted the waters by praying with his pipe so that they could wade across only knee deep. Ever since that time, they believe, there has been a rock shelf across the water at that place, and it is easily forded (Ewers 1963, 36). An unusual pipe bundle also had power. An Assinboine, Comes Out Chief, lost his six-year-old son to death. He said that because the pipe had come to him through four generations and that there was no one now to be the keeper, he wanted to give it to his son as if he had reached the age of leadership. And so the body and the pipe were wrapped together to make the sacred bundle. Never before had a bundle been made like that one. At night a bright light came from the bundle (Kennedy 1961, 11–14).

The pipe can also empower a person to face death.

In 1827 when Red Bird, chief of the Winnebago, surrendered to U.S. troops in order to save his tribe, beautifully clothed in white buckskin and carrying ceremonial pipes he advanced towards Major Whistler singing his death song: "I am ready," he said, "I do not wish to be put in irons. Let me die. I have given away my life, it is gone like that." And stooping he took a pinch of dust and blew it to the winds. "I would not take it back, it is gone." (Alexander 1967, 192)

DeSmet commented that it was a touching spectacle to see an American Indian raise the Calumet, the emblem of peace, heavenward to the Master of Life, imploring his pity (Chittenden and Richardson 1905, 2:681–82). Among the Gros Ventre a young man desiring a long life would stand crying in front of the lodge of a very old man. The old man would stand with his pipe behind the young man, both facing the direction of the rising sun and praying that his desire be fulfilled (Cooper 1940, 114). Fr. LePetit described a chief offering the first three puffs of his lighted calumet to his brother the sun and with raised hand turning from east to west to show him the direction he must take in his course (Thwaites 1896–1901, 68:127). Another ritual was to blow smoke over the bodies of people as a ritual symbol of blessing (Thwaites 1904–7, 18: 40). Any remarkable place in nature became a place of veneration and prayer. The American Indians approached curious trees, rocks, islands, mountains, caves, or waterfalls with great solemnity, smoking a pipe and leaving a little tobacco as an offering to the presiding spirit of the sacred place (West 1934, 69).

The chiefs of the Blackfoot appointed a man every four years to be in charge of the Sacred Pipes, the pipe stems, and other emblems of their religious beliefs. He lived in a special lodge that was transported by four horses. He had to undergo seven fasts, lead a celibate life, and live apart from his family, if he had one, while the public supported him for the entire term that he was the "Great Medicine." He actually had more power and exerted more influence than the civil or war chiefs. His face was always painted black (Warren 1885, 68–69).

Among the Arapaho the Flat Pipe was considered too holy to be carried on horseback or a travois. The keeper proceeded on foot. Because the bundle was two feet long and the poles about five feet, only a short distance could be covered in a day's march. When on the march, the camp formed around the keeper. During the Sun Dance the dancers touched the pipe bundle and cried over it. The women who prepared the feast honoring the Flat Pipe were amply compensated by having the privilege of seeing the pipe and touching it with their bare right feet. In another ceremony, that of "covering the pipe," the sponsor not only gained blessings for himself but also permitted others to share in this blessing at his expense because all who wished could come forward at the proper time to touch the pipe with their bare right feet. The food, which was blessed and eaten in honor of it, was is in great demand and was regarded in the same light as Holy Communion was among Christians. It was distributed among many (Carter 1938, 76–78).

Lakota medicine men journey to Green Grass on the Cheyenne River Reservation where, according to tradition, their original pipe is kept and touch their pipes to the Calf Pipe bundle. The bundle is opened on special occasions only, a ceremony through which the keeper receives his power. Martha Bad Warrior, however, opened the bundle for Wilbur Reigert, a Chippewa, in 1936 (Reigert 1975, 73) and for an anthropologist, Sidney Thomas, in 1941 (Thomas 1941). Thomas gives a detailed description of the bundle's contents. Smith describes a ceremony for the preparation of the offering clothes for the Calf Pipe (J. Smith 1964). Stanley Looking Horse told me that Green Grass is a place where all the spirits of all the medicine men who pray through the pipe are present because all their pipes are related to the Calf Pipe. Green Crass has become a place of pilgrimage for members of the American Indian movement. When I requested to pray in the presence of the Calf Pipe with my pipe in October of 1977, Looking Horse conducted a sweat lodge ceremony for me and late at night opened the small house where the Calf Pipe is kept. I felt too overwhelmed by the powerful presence of the Calf Pipe to observe any details of the bundle. Looking Horse told me that this was the first time a priest or minister had made this request and that he was pleased (Steinmetz 1990, 16).

The Sacred Pipe in Ceremony

The sacramental nature of the Sacred Pipe is most evident in its use in formal ceremonies. It is the common source from which so many ceremonies derive their sacredness. In ceremonialism one best sees the Sacred Pipe in its beauty and power. At one time it is the center of the ceremony; at another it simply makes an important contribution. Among the Lakota the Sacred Pipe must be present before a sacred ceremony begins. Although it may not be essential to Navajo ceremonialism, it brings an element of the sacred to their sand paintings.

An investigation of the Sacred Pipe pertains to

1. The transmittal of ceremonial tradition
2. The prayer to the Four Directions
3. The Sweat Lodge Ceremony
4. The Vision Quest
5. The Sun Dance
6. Ceremonies relating to death
7. Other ceremonies and dances

The Transmittal of Ceremonial Tradition

As with myth, the ceremonial life among Native Americans depended on oral tradition. Passing on this tradition was surrounded by ritual. Among the Cheyenne the pipe was filled before the repetitions of the ceremony began. "Each prayer was recited four times by the instructor and each time the learner repeated the words. After this instruction was ended, everyone smoked another long-stemmed black stone pipe" (Grinnell 1972, 2:221). Among the Comanche, there were periods of absolute silence when the pipe was passed in a circle to smoke. If the silence was broken, it was necessary to dump all the tobacco on the ground and begin anew (Wallace and Hoebel 1952, 181). A common way of announcing ceremonies among the Osage was for a messenger to go from house to house carrying in his hand a little pipe as the credential of his office (LaFlesche 1917–18, 52).

The Prayer to the Four Directions

The basic ceremony of the Sacred Pipe, which is included in all other ceremonies, is the offering of the pipe to the Four Directions. There are numerous examples of this offering ceremony from the nineteenth century (Thwaites 1904–7, 5:129–30; 24:29, 168–69; Schoolcraft 1856, 1:97) The offering and a centering prayer gather in the entire universe. The Sacred Pipe becomes the sacramental symbol of this ceremony. The ceremony can be performed without smoking the pipe but it must include the offering of tobacco in the bowl of the pipe. The offering of dry tobacco was a very widespread practice among American Indians (West 1934, 66–82).

Symbolic colors are connected with the Four Directions. After an extensive survey, Dixon concluded that "diversity and not uniformity is the characteristic feature of the symbolism, and no general principle can be laid down as underlying the choice of colors by different peoples" (Dixon 1899, 10–16). Even on a single reservation such as the Pine Ridge, Kemnitzer shows a wide variety of choice among six medicine men (1970, 71). Hodge gives a chart of colors used by ten North American tribes. These colors were used as flags placed in the Four Directions or in painting or tattooing the body and in the decoration of ceremonial objects (Hodge 1910, 1:323): "James Owen Dorsey tells us that the elements as conceived in the Indian philosophy, viz, fire, wind, water and earth, are among the Sioux tribes symbolized by the colors of the

cardinal points; and Cushing relates the same of the Zuni"
(1:325–26).

Sword, a Lakota shaman, states that in offering the
pipe to the Four Directions one is addressing the Four
Winds:

> The pipe is used because the smoke from the pipe
> smoked in communion has the potency of the feminine
> god who mediates between godkind and mankind, and
> propitiates the godkind. When a Shaman offers the pipe
> to a god, the god smokes it and is propitiated. The Four
> Winds are the akicita or messengers of the gods and in
> all ceremonies they have precedence over all the other
> gods, and for this reason should be the first addressed.
> (Walker 1917, 157)

The feminine mediating between the divine and the
human, confirmed by the myth of the Woman bringing
the Calf Pipe, is a striking example of the Lakota getting
in touch with the feminine within.

The Four Directions are prominent in the Omaha ceremony of Turning the Child. An old man stood the child
on a stone facing the east. He lifted the child by the shoul-
ders turning it to the south, the west, and the north, each
time letting its feet rest on the stone (Fletcher and
LaFlesche 1905–6, 44–45). This introduction of the child
to the cosmos was accompanied by a prayer in which all
of creation was asked to make the path of life smooth so
that the child could reach the four hills of life (childhood,
adolescence, adulthood, and old age) and beyond the four

hills to another life (115–16). Among the Osage the symbols of four valleys and four bends of a river were used (LaFlesche 1917–18, 258–59).

Finally, the number four is expressed in many ceremonial ways. A striking example is found in the Gros Ventre Sun Dance. The keeper of the Flat Pipe blew smoke from his pipe over the cottonwood tree four times and sang four songs. He then touched the tree with his pipe four times and motioned to it four times. Four times the tree moved under the efforts of the men and the influence of the pipe. The fourth time, the keeper said "now," and the tree was entirely raised up and set in the hole (Kroeber 1908, 263).

The Sweat Lodge Ceremony

The Sacred Pipe is a sacramental in the Sweat Lodge Ceremony because the participants smoke the pipe at the conclusion of the ceremony, making it a symbol and means of spiritual communion after purification. The missionary James W. Lynn claimed that the idea of purification was as deeply rooted in Dakota life as it was in that of the ancient Hebrews (1889, 171). The sweat lodge in one form or another was common to almost every tribe in the United States (Mooney 1892–93, 14:823). Black Elk, perhaps, best develops the symbolism of the Sweat Lodge and the other ceremonies with a wealth of detail (Brown 1953). The Ojibwa performed this ceremony each day for four days as an introduction into the Great Medicine Society with ceremonial smoking as part of the ceremony (Hoffman 1885–86, 204, 259). Among the Arapaho the highest of the eight Warrior Orders was that of the "Water-pouring Man" in which seven priests were the instructors of all the other orders: "Their name refers to their pouring water over the heated stones in the sweat lodge. Their ceremonies are performed in a large sweat lodge . . . which when the whole tribe was camped together, occupied the center of the circle, between the entrance and the lodge in which was kept the sacred medicine pipe" (Mooney 1892–93, 14:969).

The Piegan had the same custom (Curtis 1907–30, 6:33). The Sweat Lodge was of divine origin for the Menominee (Hoffman 1892–93, 14:92), the Omaha (Fletcher and LaFlesche 1905–6, 2: 571–78), and the Osage (LaFlesche 1917–18, 159).

The Sweat Lodge can be a ceremony in itself or it can be performed before and after another ceremony. When performed after another ceremony, its meaning is more than purification. According to Richard Moves Camp:

> It allows one to drink water and pray with the pipe to complete the ceremony. The main purpose is to untie the knot that connects the person with the sacred ceremony so that he can go from the sacred world to the profane again. He also has to live with responsibility of his vision and the concluding sweat lodge allows him to purify himself for carrying that out. (Steinmetz 1990, 58–59)

The Vision Quest

Praying with the Sacred Pipe in the Vision Quest is a sacramental of prolonged and intensive prayer. Among the Omaha, if a man's stress of feeling was great while fasting on the hill, he would leave the pipe on the ground where his appeal had been made. This form of prayer was called "addressing the pipe" (Fletcher and LaFlesche 1905–6, 2:559).

During the Vision Quest one prays to and through the spirits of animals and nature. The belief explains the great number of interesting pipe bowls with animal and bird carvings found in the Mississippi Valley mounds: hawk, heron, woodpecker, crow, beaver, otter, wildcat, rattlesnakes. The sacred nature of the pipe made pipe bowls a natural medium for these carvings (Henshaw 1880–81, 124, 150). West (1934) and Ewers (1986) both have excellent photographs of these pipe bowls. An old Lakota man explained that "a picture can be destroyed, but stone endures, so it is good that a man have the subject of his dream carved in a stone pipe that can be buried with him. Many of his possessions are left to his friends, but the sign of his dream should not be taken from him" (Densmore 1929, 80).

A vision or dream, however, could be a mixed blessing. Mooney cites the example of Black Coyote, a Sioux, who had seventy scars "arranged in various patterns of lines, circles, crosses, etc., with a long figure of the sacred pipe on one arm." He did this "in obedience to a dream as a sacrifice to save the lives of his children" (Mooney 1892–93, 14:898). At other times a person was obliged to act out his vision. Brave Buffalo passed close to the tents, imitating the actions of the elk. "Two virgins preceded him, carrying the pipe" (Densmore 1918, 17).

The Sun Dance

The Sacred Pipe is a sacramental in every phase of the Sun Dance, the only common ceremony of tribal renewal practiced by most of the Plains tribes. Leslie Spier compares the ceremonies of nineteen tribes. He states that the ceremonial use of a pipe in the Sun Dance was so general it could not be considered a specific trait of any particular tribe. It did, however, hold a more prominent place in some tribes than others (Spier 1921, 472). The Lakota were such a tribe.

> If a man's vow involved the cutting of his flesh, he was permitted to offer a pipe similar to that of the Intercessor or medicine man in charge, filled with tobacco, sealed with buffalo fat and placed beside the Intercessor's pipe during the ceremony. Lone Man stated that his Sun Dance vow included offering of a pipe; he therefore offered a pipe when fulfilling his vow and had kept the pipe with greatest care. (Densmore 1918, 103)

The preparation for the Sun Dance started with a united public declaration of all who were to dance, concluding with "to all of you [the spirits mentioned] these youths promise to present the pipe" (Deloria 1929, 389–90). When the day arrived to fulfill the Sun Dance vow, the leader held a filled pipe and prayed with the sun dancers after which the entire group smoked it (393). The leader prayed with the pipe at the cutting of the sacred tree (396–97). While the singers sang the first song, the dancers cried out, "For mysterious beings I have held the pipe; so in return I shall kill an enemy without misfortune" or "so in return I shall have horses." The sun dancer who must be pierced presents a filled pipe to someone who has been pierced previously. When the man accepts the responsibility to do the piercing, he receives a filled pipe in token and offers it ceremonially (405). Densmore adds a few additional details. "The sun dance pipe furnished by the Leader of the Dancers, was decorated at his request by one of the most skillful women of the tribe. It was considered a great honor to decorate the pipe" (Densmore 1918, 102). During the ceremony whenever "the Intercessor rose to sing or pray he held the pipe in his hand, afterwards replacing it in its ceremonial position on the altar" (127). There was a bed of fresh sage on which the buffalo skull and pipe would be laid. No one was allowed to pass between this altar and the Sun Dance tree (122). At the end of the entire ceremony the Intercessor took the main Sun Dance pipe to his lodge, broke the seal of buffalo fat, lighted the pipe, and offered it to such of his friends as felt themselves worthy to smoke it. No one who felt unworthy even dared to touch the Sun Dance Pipe (149–50). The pipe is used extensively in the present Lakota Sun Dances (Steinmetz 1990, 78–79).

Ceremonies Relating to Death

The Sacred Pipe was a sacramental in ceremonies related to death. There is an account in the *Jesuit Relations* of the burial of a Nipistingue warrior. He was seated on a hill with a gun resting on his arm, a war club in his girdle, a calumet in his mouth, a lance in his hand, a filled kettle at his side (Thwaites 1896–1901, 70: 149, 151). DeSmet also reported a burial custom. Some days after the burial the relatives of the deceased assembled to smoke over the grave. They hung presents on the nearest tree, particularly tobacco for the soul of the deceased, which is to come occasionally and smoke upon the grave. They thought that the soul was wandering not far from there until the body corrupted (27:166). The Sauk Native Americans lower the body into the grave and throw tobacco upon it. An old man is then elected to address the corpse and tell it how to reach the other world (West 1934, 79).

Fletcher describes a Keeping of the Soul Ceremony among the Lakota for a child, which took place in 1882. The pipe was accepted by the man willing to take on the responsibility of conducting it and was used throughout. A lock of hair from the deceased child was wrapped in red cloth to make the spirit bundle. The parents took care of this for the period of mourning. In the concluding feast and give-away for eight hundred people pipes were given to poor men (Fletcher 1884, 296–307).

Among the Plains Cree a braid of hair was cut off at the grave and tied to the end of a stick which was placed at the head of the grave. On the fourth night after the death the braid of hair was taken to a feast by the man who cut it off. He smoked the pipe, addressed a prayer to the Creator, and "successively pointed the pipe to those spirit powers whose duty it was to care for the souls of the dead and petitioned their aid" (Mandelbaum 1940, 249). According to Winnebago tradition, not only food but a pipe and tobacco are given to the spirit of the deceased person so that it may offer them to the spirits it meets on the road and make requests of them. These gifts are called "spiritual" tobacco and food (Radin 1915–16, 141–42). Even today presenting spiritual food is an important ceremony among the Lakota on the Pine Ridge Reservation (Steinmetz 1990, 51–53).

Among the Chippewa when a person was unable to keep up with the nomadic travel through old age, there seemed to be two alternatives: one was to leave him behind to starve; the other was to inflict death upon him. In one account a sweat lodge was prepared as in the ceremony of adoption. While the person was in the preparatory ceremony, the family rejoiced that the Master of Life had told them how to dispose of the aged and infirm by "sending them to a better country, where they will be renovated and hunt again with all the vigor of youth. They then smoke the pipe of peace and have their dog feast; they also sing the grand medicine song." When the songs and the dances are repeated, a son gives his father a death blow with the tomahawk. They paint his body in the best manner and bury it with a war weapon (Thwaites 1904–7, 2:110–11).

Other Ceremonies and Dances

The sacramental nature of the Sacred Pipe can be seen from many other ceremonies and dances. The Omaha had the ritual of the White Buffalo Hide, a ceremony which reenacted the creation of the buffalo and every aspect of the hunt. The first song was "The Pipe Appears":

> The holy pipe
> Holy, I say
> The Holy pipe, behold you.

The second song, which preceded the actual smoking of the pipe, commanded men to take the pipe to pray:

> Now I bid you.
> Within your lips take this holy pipe, holy pipe.
> The pipe, it appears, appears before you I say.
> Now I bid you.
> Within your lips take this holy pipe, holy pipe.
> The pipe it appears, appears before you, I say.

The following reflections on the songs are made. In the first song the pipe "appears" not by any agency of man but by its own power and commands men to behold.... Although so simple and concrete, this song throws more light on the native thought and belief in the use of the pipe than any single song the writer has found.... In the second song the music is echoed, but it is treated in a way to suggest the movement toward the pipe, which in the first song stood apart, clothed with mysterious power. It now comes near and in touch with the supplicants. . . . These two songs complement each other and show both dramatic and musical form (Fletcher and LaFlesche 1905–6, 286–89).

The pipe was used in Sioux ceremonies to honor brave deeds. Sometimes a modern hero's name was put into a song in the place of the old one (Fletcher 1892, 135–44). The pipe was used in many dances. Catlin relates that a filled pipe was passed around during a Mandan dance at a buffalo feast that involved ritual sexual intercourse (Catlin 1967, 70–71). In the Mandan Buffalo Bull Dance the pipe was used ritually against evil forces by pointing it at a dancer in a frightening costume who represented the evil spirit (59–60). The Menominee used the pipe in their Rain Dance, which was performed during times of prolonged drought. The ceremony concluded with the smoking of four long pipes that rested beside the drum (Skinner 1915, 206–8). They also held a Tobacco Dance to reenact the myth in which tobacco was obtained (211–12).

Among the Plains Cree the ceremony that ranked next to the Sun Dance was the Smoking Tipi Ceremony. It was also given to fulfill a vow. "The ceremony consisted of a night-long singing session during which many prayers were said, offerings given, and pipes ritualistically manipulated" (Mandelbaum 1940, 272). There was also the Masked Dance.

The pledger carried a staff with deer hoofs attached. He went from tipi to tipi and shook his staff over the heads of those men whom he wished to join him in the dance. As he did this he spoke in inverted fashion saying, "I do not want you." The men so chosen followed the pledger into his tipi. There he offered up a pipe, rotating it in a counter-clockwise direction instead of clockwise as was done in every other ritual. (274)

The Chippewa had a "drum religion" that they received from the Sioux and passed on to the Menominee (Densmore 1913, 142–73). The main purpose was to establish peace between people who had been at enmity (142). A Menominee chief said:

I will keep the drum in my house. There will always be tobacco beside it and the drum pipe will always be filled. When I smoke at home, I will use the pipe that belongs to the drum. My friends will come to my house to visit the drum and we will ask the drum to strengthen us in our faith and resolution to live justly and to wrong no one. (143)

A small ceremony with singers usually takes place every fourth night. The presentation of a drum to another tribe involves an elaborate ceremony with a feast and a return of suitable gifts for the drum.

The Gros Ventre were given a Feathered Pipe by the Thunder God during a violent thunderstorm (Cooper 1957, 4). They conducted an annual rite with this pipe primarily to pray both for rain and for protection against storms and floods. Before the ceremony, the pipe was taken to the sweat lodge (149). The keeper had to have two wives. Because the pipe was never left unattended, one wife had to sleep outside the tipi during her menses. The Feathered Pipe was considered a brother to Pipe Child, usually a daughter of the keeper (135). The pipe was related to their sacred Flat Pipe that belonged to the ground, whereas the Feathered Pipe belonged above the earth (77).

The Crow conducted a ceremony for the planting of tobacco during which the pipe was smoked. "Sometimes a man may be afraid to smoke the pipe for fear that if the tobacco should not grow, some great harm would befall him. . . . The act of smoking is regarded as a ceremonial equivalent to the sacrifice of the life of the smoker that the tobacco plant may grow" (Simms 1904, 332).

The Lakota brought the pipe into the Ghost Dance of 1890. A woman "remained standing near the tree throughout the dance, holding a sacred redstone pipe stretched out towards the west, the direction from which the messiah was to appear" (Mooney 1892–93, 14:823–24). Among the Arapaho the opening Ghost Dance song was on the pipe:

> O my children! O my children!
> Here is another of your pipes,
> Look! thus I shouted,
> Look! thus I shouted,

When I moved the earth,
When I moved the earth.

"By 'another pipe' is probably meant the newer revelation
of the messiah, the pipe being an important feature of all
sacred ceremonies, and all their previous religious traditions having centered about the . . . flat pipe" (958–59). In
other words, a new religious movement as important as
the Ghost Dance would be immediately associated with
the Sacred Pipe.

S. A. Barrett states that in the Dream Dance of the
Chippewa and Menominee "a special pipe, together with
both of its stems, always accompanied the drum." (1911,
273). The Osage used a pipe to consecrate a new shrine
that contained sacred animal skins, the symbolic objects
through which they prayed to the Great Spirit. First,
songs of the symbolic pipe and the ritual of the discovery
of tobacco were sung. Then the priest blew a whiff of
smoke on the rush-mat shrine, which contained the animal
skins, a strap with an eagle's leg and scalp attached to it,
and a ceremonial pipe with its tobacco pouch (LaFlesche
1927–28, 725). A Hidatsa shrine contained the skulls of
two medicine men, who were formally thought to be ea-
gles, and a pipe. A myth explains how the skulls and
pipe became the tribal medicine (Pepper and Wilson 1907,
284–94).

The Chief and the Sacred Pipe

The Sacred Pipe was a sacramental in political life. A chief used it in the exercise of many of his functions, making his position a religious and a political one. There was no separation of Church and State among the Native Americans. The use of the Sacred Pipe today among members of the American Indian movement gives a religious characteristic to their political activity.

Among the Poncas the head chief had his special pipe, and he was the only one who could make chiefs. No man was a chief until he had smoked the Sacred Pipe (Howard 1965, 90). Dorsey states:

> The sacred pipes were feared by all except those who are to be made chiefs. . . . The women and children stay outside or back of the circle, as they are afraid of the pipes. Even the horses are sent to the rear. When the chiefs elect enter the large tent, they give many horses to the retiring chiefs. Then, they put the pipes to their mouths and inhale the smoke, for if they should refuse to inhale it, they would die very soon thereafter, before the end of the year.
>
> Inside the pipes are laid on a bed of wild sage near the Sacred Buffalo Skull. All the chiefs paint their faces and other parts of their bodies red and wear buffalo robes in imitation of the buffalo. The pipes are handed to the candidates and they are given instructions. (J. Dorsey 1881–82, 359–60)

Schoolcraft states:

> If a chief is anxious to know the disposition of his
> people towards him, or if he wishes to settle any differ-
> ences between them, he announces his intention of
> opening his medicine bag and smoking his sacred stem;
> and no man who entertains a grudge against any of the
> party thus assembled can smoke with the sacred stem;
> as that ceremony dissipates all differences and is never
> violated. (1856, 5:170)

In reparation for a murder of a Blackfoot two Cree chiefs
made excuses to the government agent responsible for
maintaining peace. They gave him a horse and a couple of
very beautiful pipes, one a Calumet adorned with feathers
and green horse hair (Thwaites 1904–7, 23:107). Among
the Cheyenne a chief was expected to exercise the greatest
self-control. When one chief heard that his wife was being
chased by another man, he became very angry. He seized
his pipe, however, smoked, and renewed his pledge not to
say any harsh words. If he had weakened, he would have
been despised by his People. The smoking of the pipe
almost always worked (Llewellyn and Hoebel 1941, 79).
Sweet Medicine, a Cheyenne culture hero, told their chief:
"You chiefs are peace makers. Although your son might
be killed in front of your tipi you should take a peace
pipe and smoke. Then you will be called an honest chief"
(Stands in Timber and Liberty 1967, 44). Among the
Omaha war plans were kept secret because a chief would

try to dissuade a leader from organizing a war party by bestowing presents on him (J. Dorsey 1881–82, 315–17). Among the Iroquois chiefs "to smoke together" was almost synonymous with "holding council" (Fenton 1953, 155). Among the Coeur D'Alene each degree of authority was determined by the type of pipe one had. The chiefs of a band had a "Band Pipe," the chiefs of a division, a "Chief Pipe," and the chief of the tribe, the "Tribal Pipe." In making agreements if a Band Pipe was smoked, it was only binding on the band to whom the pipe belonged. When the Tribal Pipe was smoked, however, it was binding on the entire tribe (Teit 1927–28, 154).

The Omaha opened no councils without the chiefs who were the keepers of the pipes (J. Dorsey 1881–82, 358). The Sacred Pipe was very much involved in their entire social structure. The Honga gens was the source of the Sacred Pipes and had a right to all the pipes as that gens had the first authority. Peace Pipes, however, were given to the gens that formed the Council of the Seven Chiefs. An Omaha legend relates how they were given out. The pipe bearers passed by the first gens because they were engaged in ceremonies pertaining to the taking of life. Even to this day the other gens remind them: "You are no people; you have no peace pipe." The pipe bearers gave pipes to the other gens to give them authority to perform their respective duties, such as the election of chiefs, the management of war councils, the direction of the people in hunting, and the maintenance of peace. Each gens had its pipe, but there was one pipe belonging to the leading chiefs, and they prayed with it to bring punishment on the men who caused trouble in the tribe (Fletcher and LaFlesche 1905–6, 48).

Among the Arapaho the Tribal Council met in the large tipi in which the keeper of the Sacred Pipe dwelt. The chiefs spent most of their time there when the tribe was encamped. Taking down the sacred tipi was the signal for moving camp (Hilger 1952, 193).

Another important social function of the pipe was the administration of oaths (Hilger 1952, 103–4). The Hopi considered ceremonial smoking "a signature put into the other with smoke." Any material paper agreement could be burned, destroyed, or stolen, but a signature by smoke was a sacred oath that would never be broken (Waters 1963, 275). The pipe was used in the Cheyenne legal system. Through the pipe, people's differences were worked out by deferring to another's judgment and not simply by handing down a verdict (Llewellyn and Hoebel 1941, 339).

The Sacred Pipe in the Societies

The societies were an important part of the social fabric of Native American life. They gave, especially to men, identity, social role, and prestige. The sacramental use of the Sacred Pipe sanctified these areas of life.

The Oglala Lakota had the Tokala or Kit Fox Society, whose members were supposed to be as active and wily on the warpath as this little animal. Besides two leaders there were two pipe bearers. The pipe bearers apparently presided over the formal meetings. On the war path one of them filled the pipe just before going out to charge the enemy, leaving the bowl and taking the stem. If they killed the enemy without harm, the stem was joined to the bowl and smoked. If they were killed, the filled pipe bowl separated from the stem was a symbol of death. The ritual action was also done because they believed that the stem would bring the party back to the bowl in the camp. The lance bearers in this society took the lead in battle and seldom retreated. Because some believed that to accept this position was certain death, the installation was a solemn event. When there was a vacancy, one of the pipe bearers informed the candidate, who had been invited to a formal meeting not knowing its purpose or his fate. Because the candidate usually hesitated, the herald shouted out his virtues, the women cheered, and the members sang songs of the glory and fate of former lance bearers. A favorite song was "I am a *tokala*. I am living in uncertainty." In the end the candidate usually accepted to avoid public disgrace. The pipe man then lectured the candidate on his responsibilities. The candidate's relatives gave gifts to the needy (Wissler 1912, 14–20).

The Lakota Miwatani Society pipe bearers quieted quarrels. The pipe was taken to the scene of the quarrel and smoked as a peace pipe. If a member of the society was the direct cause of the quarrel, he was expelled from the society (Wissler 1912, 47). The Silent Eaters Society was a feast and dancing association. In this case, however, there was no singing and dancing but only silent eating. After the feast, their conversations were about war deeds. They concluded with a pipe offering (75). The pipes used in these societies were consecrated by a medicine man. This involved four sweat lodge ceremonies. He prayed over the pipe, filled it with tobacco and sealed it with the fat from the heart of the buffalo, and wrapped it in wolf skin. Now it was a Medicine Pipe or a Sacred Pipe. From that moment on it was taken care of by a pipe bearer (54).

Among the Crows was a Black Mouth or Soldier Society. The two officers took care of a flat-stemmed pipe, red on one side and black on the other, decorated with quill work and a dyed horsetail. They were expected to adjust quarrels and preserve peace. The black and red colors symbolized night and day, bad and good will. All the spirits were represented by the pipe. Members prayed to the pipe that their children should grow up and asked it for plenty of buffalo (Lowie 1913, 275–76).

The Blackfoot had a society of medicine men who had an all-smoking ceremony. It was a kind of medicine counting coup. Like warriors recalling deeds they counted the different medicine rituals they had owned and sang the songs connected with them (Wissler 1913, 445–46). The Sarsi had a dancing organization called the Dogs Society. The pipes were obtained by a payment of ten horses from the previous leaders. They kept order during the Sun Dance (Goddard 1914, 467–68).

The Plains Ojibwa had a society for healing and exorcizing demons. They wore rags and hideous masks. One time a band of Sioux came across a group of them who were dancing instead of fleeing. The Sioux thought that they were spirits and sat down on the grass to watch their crazy antics. The Sioux filled their pipes and addressed them as spirits. The Ojibwa, however, pulled out guns from behind their clothes and killed the Sioux and fled (Skinner 1914, 502).

It was formerly the custom for a man who was given the right to do so by a dream to proclaim a public confession of illicit sexual intercourse. Everyone was obliged to abstain from sexual relations for four days. Anyone violating the taboo attended the meeting with a face painted half black. The pipe was never passed to this person (Skinner 1914, 506–7).

Among the Pawnee the pipe was used in the ceremony for making lances (Murie 1914, 564, 567). Among the Winnebago the Medicine Dance Society had a ritual whose purpose was to strengthen the powers obtained in a vision. The pipe invocation started in the east (Radin 1911, 149–208). The Omaha had the Hae-thus Society (the name untranslatable), which spread to the Oto, the Iowa, and the Pawnee. The Sioux adopted it and called it the Omaha Dance or Grass Dance. The society had its special pipe. Its purpose was to decide whose brave deeds would be preserved in song. "Without this consent of the society none would dare allow a song to be composed in his honor. . . . These songs preserved for generations the deeds of the members and, therefore, to a good degree told the story of the tribe itself" (Fletcher 1892, 135–44).

Among the Fox when one was reluctant to join a society or to become its leader, members sometimes captured the candidate by force and held his hand around the pipe. Once his hand touched the pipe, he could not refuse (Hilger 1952, 121). If any man of high rank was unwilling to participate in the Arapaho Dog Dance because of the restrictions involved, the same procedure was followed (Kroeber 1902–7, 200).

The Sacred Pipe in Peace and War

The Sacred Pipe was the sacramental means by which war was declared and fought and peace was established. It is a striking example of the ambivalence of a religious symbol. Probably the best-known and most widely distributed dances among the Native Americans were the Calumet Dance and those related to it: the Pawnee Hako Ceremony (Fletcher 1900–1901), the Omaha Pipe Dance (Fletcher 1884), the Sioux Hunkyapi Ceremony (Densmore 1918, 68–77) and the Iroquois Eagle Dance (Fenton 1953, 13–153). William N. Fenton establishes the common relationship between these dances (178–79). The purpose was to bless the individual with children and long life, to make relatives, and to establish peace between individuals and tribes.

The Calumet was not properly the pipe but a highly ornamented and symbolic stem. Among the southeastern tribes" the stem used in peace-making ceremony remained with the chief who had received the embassy while the pipe bowl was taken out and carried back by the visitors" (Swanton 1946, 547). Among the Pawnee the word *hako* means "breathing mouth of wood" and refers to the two wands or stems that represent the pipe. A detailed description clearly shows that the Hako were the famous Calumet (Fletcher 1900–1901, 40). This description is very similar to that found in the Siouan tribes (J. Dorsey 1881–82, 277) and to the comparative descriptions of the Osage, Omaha, Ponca, and Pawnee (LaFlesche 1939, 253–55). The Hako stems represented both the female and male elements whose every detail was symbolic and of greater importance than the pipe (Fletcher 1900–1901, 287–88, 295–96).

"In fact, for certain uses no pipe was attached to the stem, and instead the head of a duck, woodcock or of some other bird was supplied" (West 1934, 231). Although the decorated stem was the central object, a catlinite bowl was frequently attached among the Seneca as was also done in the Pawnee Hako Ceremony (Fenton 1953, 155). Among the Omaha these stems normally had no bowls and were used as Peace Pipes only when regular pipes were not available (Fletcher 1884, 309). Regular pipes with large catlinite bowls used in peace councils were also called Calumets (Denig 1928–29, 446). Among the Assiniboine, although the pipe was never omitted, the real Calumet was never opened except in dealing with strangers (448). The term *Calumet* had shifting meanings.

The deeper meaning of the Calumet Dance was not merely to establish peace between two groups of people but "to make a sacred kinship," which was the basis of the peace (J. Dorsey 1881–82, 276). The Calumet was not only the sign of friendship but, even more, an object that had the power to compel acceptance. Schoolcraft states: "It was always considered hazardous to the chief himself to refuse it; as it is supposed that such a refusal exposes

him to an angry visitation of the Great Spirit, in taking
away the life of the chief or some of his family. The pipe
bearer is always received." (1856, 3:263)

Among the Hurons the relatives of a murdered person
demanded presents from the tribe of the guilty person.
This tribe gave the Hurons a pipe to smoke because they
believed that there was "nothing as suitable as tobacco to
appease the passions." The relatives of the deceased received as many as forty presents (Thwaites 1896–1901,
10:219). In another case a chief lit his pipe and smoked.
He dug a hole in the ground in which they buried the war
axe and professed to deposit all their ill feelings with it
(Thwaites 1904–7, 27:136).

Jesuit missionaries summarized the importance of the
Calumet as a "passport and safeguard to enable one to go
in safety everywhere, no one daring to injure in any manner those who bear this caduceus [*sic*]. It had only to be
displayed and life is secure, even in the thickest of the
fight." The Jesuit Fr. Marquette had an occasion to experience this. Fr. Marquette showed his Calumet but

> the Indians were ready to pierce him with arrows from
> all sides when God suddenly touched the heart of the
> old man standing at water's edge. No doubt it was
> through the sight of the Calumet, which they did not
> clearly distinguish from afar . . . but as I did not cease
> displaying it, they were influenced by it and checked
> the ardor of the young men. (Thwaites 1896–1901,
> 59:151)

Among the northwestern tribes, including the Nez Perce, Blackfeet, Snake, and Walla Walla, the fur traders had to establish peace among them for the sake of good business. On one occasion there was a peace negotiation between the American Indians and a band of fur traders during which some hundreds of the traders' pipes were given away. Finally, terms of peace were agreed upon and there was the most profound silence over the group until the Peace Pipe had six times gone around the circle of the assembly (Ross 1956, 161, 123).

DeSmet describes the presentation of the Calumet after a dance among the Coeur d'Alenes. The head of the pipe rested on the breast of one woman and the stem handsomely decorated with feathers on the breast of another. The most distinguished persons preceded the calumet bearers (Chittenden and Richardson 1905, 2:581). He also describes Little Chief giving a horse and a robe decorated with porcupine quills to establish peace with a much-hated enemy. He threw the robe on him on the spot and lit the Peace Pipe to seal the agreement. The pipe made several rounds, being smoked in thanksgiving (599). Another chief ordered his kettle to be filled with his three fattest dogs in DeSmet's honor as they smoked the Calumet (Thwaites 1904–7, 27:136).

Frances Densmore gives a dramatic description of a peace council between the Chippewa and the Sioux.

In each camp was the sound of singing and of shrill war cries; excitement was in the air and it seemed that an

encounter instead of a truce was in preparation. . . .
The Chippewa were led by . . . one bearing the pipe,
followed by four women. . . . To and fro in front of the
warriors walked the women. Often it was only their
presence that prevented violence. . . . All sang as they
came forward. The melody was the same in both tribes
but the Chippewa sang the names of the Sioux leaders
and the Sioux the names of the Chippewa leaders, each
praising the valor of the other. . . . Then the side which
had asked for peace sent forward its pipe bearer. Holding the pipe in his hands, he offered the stem in turn to
the opposing leaders, each of whom puffed the pipe.
Then the other tribe sent forward its pipe bearer in the
same manner the two tribes camped near each other for
some time and social dances were held every
night. (Densmore 1913, 127–29)

M. W. Beckwith described a peace ceremony between
two hostile tribes. Two old men came forward each representing a tribe. The representative of the tribe attacked
smoked first and handed the pipe to the representative of
the aggressor tribe, who passed it on to each person in the
lodge. White visitors were allowed to stroke the pipe instead of smoking it. The aggressor tribe chose a young
boy to whom each of the old men gave a piece of meat,
laying it upon his tongue so that the boy did not touch it
with his hands. Afterward he was given a drink. Both the
meat and the drink had been "made medicine" by the
medicine man (Beckwith 1930, 424–25). DeSmet followed this same instinct, acting as a peace maker. He
urged the Sioux to make presents to the children of those

Potawatomies whom they had killed, which is called covering the dead, and to smoke the Calumet (Chittenden and Richardson 1905, 1:190).

Edwin T. Denig describes in detail the exact manner of handling their pipe in a peace council among the tribes of the Upper Missouri (Denig 1928–29, 446–47). Catlin called the Peace Pipe the "most inviolable pledge that they can possibly give" (1841, 1:235). DeSmet called the Calumet "the solemn pledge of peace, the token of Indian brotherhood, the most formal declaration of entire forgiveness and sincere pardon of injury" (Chittenden and Richardson 1905, 2:519). Occasionally, however, the pipe was used as a means of deception, but this was rare (Thwaites 1896–1901, 68:195).

There was a way to free oneself in a symbolic way from the obligation of the pipe: "In October, while the Ghost Dance was being organized at his camp, Sitting Bull had deliberately broken "the pipe of peace" which he had kept in his house since his surrender in 1881, and when asked why he had broken it, replied that he wanted to die and to fight" (Mooney 1892–93, 14:854–55).

To refuse the pipe was one way of declaring one's warlike inclination. DeSmet had every reason to worry one time when the Pawnees departed suddenly, refusing to smoke the Calumet (Thwaites 1904–7, 27, 208).

But there was also a War Pipe. Bartram spoke of the red-painted Calumet being used as a war standard. In peace negotiations it was displayed new, clean, and painted white (Swanton 1924–25, 435). Marquette observed the same dual use (Thwaites 1896–1901, 59:129,

131). The southeastern American Indians hung a Calumet
of War in their council lodge during war deliberations
(Swanton 1946, 699). I have already mentioned the
Hatchet Pipe, which could be used either to kill a person
or to smoke (McGee 1893–94, 172).

Among the Omaha the keeper of the Tent of War
called the Seven Chiefs for war deliberations. If war was
declared, the chiefs smoked the pipe associated with the
keeper. "This was a religious act and through it the decision became sanctified. . . . The organization of volunteer
war parties generally followed this authorization." It was
usually done through the warrior societies. A person of
some prominence sent a pipe to the leaders of each of the
principal societies. If the leaders sanctioned the enterprise,
they themselves smoked and presented the pipe to the
members of their societies at their next meeting, and all
who smoked engaged themselves by that very act to join.
No one was obliged to smoke against his will (Fletcher
and LaFesche 1905–6, 142).

The Lakota had a black pipe used as a War Pipe. On
the warpath the shaman held the pipe, chewed medicine
that was blessed in a special ceremony and carried in wolf
skins, and blew it into the air, making it misty and dense,
a wolf's day. As a result, they approached the enemy un-
seen and took his horses away. When the enemy went out
to look for the horses, they were killed (Walker 1982, 95).

The War Pipe could unite many diverse tribes. The
brother of the Kiowa Pushing Bear had been killed at the
Timber Mountain Sun Dance of 1867. He sent the pipe
around to summon a large war party. Through the influ-

ence of the pipe he was able to unite the Kiowa, Apache, Comanche, Cheyenne, Arapaho, Osage, and Crow tribes (Mooney 1895–96, 297). Among the Osage the council during time of war selected a man to act as mediator between the People and the Great Spirit. The pipe, containing the prayers of the People, was solemnly filled and placed in his hands. The keeper went alone into the hills where he thought only of the prayers of the People and cried continuously, carrying in his hand the Prayer Pipe and fasting for seven days (LaFlesche 1927–28, 579). Among the Cheyenne when war parties were undertaken on foot, the men who carried the pipe were the leaders (Grinnell 1972, 2:8). Among the Fox an old man stayed at home and guarded the pipe and sang songs to the spirit of the owl while one of the warriors in the party carried the Sacred Owl Pack (Michaelson 1921, 19, 21).

Sometimes the pipe was used for divination. Every evening the Chippewa warriors sat in a row, facing the enemy's territory. The leader took his drum, sang, and lit his pipe. "As he sang the leader shook his rattle of deer hoofs or laid it besides the pipe and looked away towards the enemy's country while his silent warriors waited on divination" (Densmore 1913, 94).

The pipe was also used to honor men renowned in war. The pipe was brought to a man. If he thought himself entitled to the honor and was ready to accept it, he took the pipe. If he thought others were braver than himself, he refused it (Kroeber 1908, 251).

Another use of the pipe was related to scalps. Before instruction to a Cheyenne on how to treat the scalp of an enemy, the pipe was filled, lit and held toward the sky and the ground and then toward the scalp with a prayer asking for further good fortune (Grinnell 1972, 37). The Plains Cree had a Sacred Pipe Stem Dance before war to pray for an abundant harvest of scalps and a greater number of horses (Skinner 1914, 536). Radin gives the lengthy prayers of the Winnebago War-Bundle feast. Its primary purpose was an invocation for success in war, but it developed into a general ceremony for thanksgiving to the spirits. An important part of the ceremony was the four fillings of the pipe and the smoking ritual (Radin 1915–16, 427–71).

The Sacred Pipe as a Sacramental
for All Needs

The Sacred Pipe was a sacramental that sanctified almost every life situation. One of its major uses was in healing. When the Chippewa dug for medicine herbs, they offered the pipe every place they took a herb (Hilger 1951, 90). The Arapaho medicine men used the pipe to cure rattlesnake bites (Hilger 1952, 129–30). When the usual remedies failed, the relatives of the sick person promised some personal sacrifice to obtain health, such as taking part in the Sun Dance, offering a part of a finger, fasting in isolation or offering material to the Sacred Pipe for recovery. He provided food for a feast, and the distinguished warriors were invited. Each warrior recounted four coups before a pipe was lit. A green cherry branch was greased and put into the fire to light the pipe. If it burnt well, the man would recover, but if poorly, he was afraid. Then, the pipe was smoked in great silence (Kroeber 1902–7 272).

The missionary Gideon Pond observed a Sioux ceremony. Everyone offered prayers at the back of the medicine man, who was officiating between them and the god. Mothers fixed the little mouths of the unconscious infants carefully and reverently on the stem of the consecrated pipe, which the medicine man extended to them backward over his shoulder (Pond 1860–67, 243). The Sacred Pipe still is prominent among the Plains tribes today.

The Sacred Pipe was the ceremonial method of requesting any favor of importance. Accepting the pipe and smoking it was a favorable answer (Grinnell 1972, 2:11). In a Natchez marriage when the parties of both the bride and the groom agreed, the future husband went on a hunt and brought back sufficient food for the feast. The two families contracted the alliance. They all assembled at the house of the girl's parents. They served the pair, who ate from the same dish. After the meal, the bridegroom smoked the pipe with the parents of the bride and then with his own parents (Thwaites 1897–   , 68:141). The pipe was also used during marital difficulties in later years. When a man ran off with another's wife, he found the ceremonial grandfather of the husband. He gave him a pipe and two or three horses. The old man took the pipe, the horses, and the wife to the husband. The man was obliged to do no violence nor to get angry. If he took the pipe, the wife was free. Sometimes, however, he decided to keep her. He, then, might cut off the tip of her nose, slash her cheek, or cut off her hair (Curtis 1907–30,

6:149). The pipe was used in broader community relations. In later days when two or three families wished
to move to another part of the reservation, pipes were
exchanged with the new neighbors. The pipe was given
to the one with whom they wished to establish friendship by giving a horse or a feast (J. Dorsey 1893–94,
235–36).

The pipe was the center of the hunt. A Cheyenne
medicine man, holding a pipe painted red over bowl and
stem, walked to the opening of a chute which would force
the antelope to fall into a pit. Then he walked onto the
prairie singing sacred songs and held up his pipe to the
Great Spirit (Grinnell 1972, 1:280). The pipe bearer was
the man in charge of the Oglala hunt. Four pipe bearers
announced the moving of the camp and the direction of
travel. They led the procession to where the buffalo were.
A scout on returning took a whiff of the pipe. If he said
he had seen many buffalo, the akicita, those keeping order
in front and back, would go to the top of the hill and see.
The pipe men considered the situation, the direction of
the wind, and so on, and gave instructions. The akicita
saw to it that no one attacked alone and would punish any
violator by striking him senseless and cutting up his tipi
(Wissler 1912, 8–9). Another Lakota practice was to place
a buffalo skull, usually with red paint and sometimes decorated with feathers and quill work, in the council tipi.
The shaman who had the vision relative to the chase held
the pipe with the stem pointing to the north, east, south,
and west, the heaven, and the earth. The pipe was smoked
and offered to the skull of the buffalo and the Spirit of the

Buffalo was called upon to give aid in a successful hunt (Walker 1982, 75–76).

Among the Arapaho the pipe was also used in the lighter moments of entertainment which consisted in a contest of telling true stories.

> A pipe passed around and smoked during the contest serves to cause the truth to be told. Those who are present deny or affirm a man's statements about himself. Sometimes a man when thus challenged will at once give a horse to a doubter in order to prove his manliness. At other times, statements are challenged in joke especially between brothers-in-law. (Kroeber 1902–7, 318–19)

The pipe was used by ceremonial contraries too. They grabbed meat out of boiling water.

> When the one who is to offer this sacrifice takes the pipe to the priest in charge of the ceremony and asks for instructions, the pipe is reversed. That is the stem is fixed in the bowl of the pipe and the hole which commonly received the stem is filled with the smoking material. (Grinnell 1972, 2:131)

The Sacred Pipe as the Symbolic Man

Because the Sacred Pipe is sacramental, it is, of course, symbolic, standing for a reality beyond itself. This sense of the symbolic meaning was, perhaps, best achieved among the Osage. They achieved tribal unity between two divisions by considering the pipe as the "symbolic man." During an address the words "I am a person who has verily made a pipe of his body" meant symbolically that the "pipe is the life symbol of his people" (LaFlesche 1914–15). It was not the pipe itself but its meaning that was important to the Osage.

> Contrasted with the Omaha pipes, that of the Osage looks crude as to finish, but the appearance of these symbolic articles bears no special significance, for it is the spirit of the ceremony and its aim that has the most important place in the minds of the people. An Omaha said to Miss Fletcher when she was studying the *Wawon* ceremony in 1883: "So great is the affection and respect we feel for these pipes that were we to see them imitated in corn husk we would show them honor." By this he meant that it is the teaching of the rite and not the actual pipes, which are employed as symbols, that are reverenced by the people. (LaFlesche 1939, 252)

The Sacred Pipe and Christianity

The religious meaning of the Sacred Pipe and its sacramental use has been influenced by Christianity far more than most anthropologists are willing to admit. The two most widely quoted Lakota on their religion are Sword, who was an ordained Episcopal deacon, and Black Elk, who was a Catholic catechist. These two men are frequently quoted without any consideration of the possible influence of Christianity on their Lakota thinking. In recent years on the Pine Ridge Reservation in South Dakota I discovered a Christian re-interpretation of Lakota symbols in the religious imagination of one generation of Lakota (Steinmetz 1990, 176–91). The Sacred Pipe has even been a sacramental in Christian ceremony. I do not suggest that there was not a pre-Christian theology of the Sacred Pipe that explained its spiritual meaning as Paper claims. There are aboriginal concepts distinct from Christian ones and this distinction remains even after a relationship between the two traditions is made. From my twenty years of experience on the Pine Ridge Reservation, however, I disagree with him that the recent modifications are "a Native means of responding to Christian domination in order to preserve Native spirituality" and that "the recent modifications are merely a "Christian overlay" (Paper 1988, 58). At least in one generation of Lakota medicine men and serious thinkers, discovering a genuine relationship between the two traditions was not used as a polemic to make their Lakota religion more acceptable, nor was it superficial. An exploration of the relationship between these two religious traditions was made in a dialogue that lasted several years among the priests and medicine men on the Rosebud Reservation in South Dakota. William Stolzman, one of the priests involved, presents some very interesting conclusions (1986).

In the mid-nineteenth century DeSmet described a Flathead praying during the night. Before prayer he raked out a live coal. When the prayers were finished, preceded and followed by the sign of the cross, he smoked his Calumet and went to bed. He did this three or four times a night (Thwaites 1904–7, 27:291). Fr. Allonez wrote in 1674 that when the American Indians at Green Bay, Wisconsin, "pass the church they throw tobacco all around it, as a token of respect to the Greatest Divinity of whom they ever heard" (West 1934, 67). It is significant that the early Jesuit missionaries did not include the pipe among the "diabolical objects" that had to be destroyed. Remembering a sermon that all medicine bundles must be given up, a young man gathered all of them and took them to the chapel. When the priest arrived, he held a feast. He told the American Indians that because the bundles were keeping the devil among them, they should be burned. The priest made them a present of tobacco and each one lit his Calumet, threw fire into the "impious implements," thanked God together, sang a hymn, and went away contented (Thwaites 1896–1901, 24: 137). An old man told me at Pine Ridge that some of the old men would try to light their pipes from candles on the altar at the offertory time and were chased away by the priest.

There have been more recent influences on the pipe. D. B. Shimkin states that the contact of Shoshone and Christian traditions led to a profound reorientation of the Sun Dance (1953, 458). Both Fred W. Voget (1953, 496–97) and Åke Hultkrantz, (1969, 36–38) elaborate on the Christian reinterpretation of Shoshone symbols in this ceremony. In the Ute Sun Dance the tree was raised on the third attempt instead of the fourth. "This is an illustration of how the old Plains sacred number has been replaced by the Christian number three" (Jones 1955, 247). This reinterpretation has continued in recent years with medicine men on the Pine Ridge Reservation. For George Plenty Wolf the effigy of the rawhide man hanging from the Sun Dance tree represented the return of Christ, the buffalo effigy, the Old Testament, and the man effigy, the New Testament. The piercing of the flesh was a reminder of the piercing of Jesus (Steinmetz 1990, 189–90). During a Mass that followed the Sun Dance on the grounds at Pine Ridge, South Dakota, Edgar Red Cloud held the pipe and sang a Sun Dance song during the Holy Communion part of the Mass. He also related the Lakota and Christian traditions by saying that "when the Indians knew Mother Earth, they knew the Blessed Virgin Mary but they did not know her by name. And the Woman who brought the Calf Pipe is the Blessed Virgin." Pete Catches said that he prays with his pipe in memory of his vision as the priest changes bread and wine into the Body and Blood of Christ in memory of the Last Supper (190–91).

The Sacred Pipe has been a sacramental in Christian ceremony. In a chapel at Oglala, South Dakota, a mural depicts the Trinity in Lakota symbols. A tipi in which the water bird dives into the depths to get earth so that the Great Spirit can make humans expresse God the Father in creation, a Native American featured as Christ on the cross expresses God the Son in redemption, and a thunder bird with twelve tongues expresses God the Holy Spirit in sanctification. A pipe below the crucifix represents man offering himself to the Trinity (Collins 1969). In addition,

I frequently prayed with the Sacred Pipe at funerals and on other occasions.

Finally, the Sacred Pipe is a sacramental in the Half Moon fireplace of the Native American Church on the Pine Ridge Reservation. They use four ceremonial cigarettes during their ceremony. In their minds the cigarette represents the pipe because the Lakota word for pipe, *canunpa,* instead of the one for smoke, *canli,* is used. At times the actual pipe was used in the early days by the old man, Red Bear, and George Gap and in recent years by Solomon Red Bear (Steinmetz 1990, 94–96, 144). In 1974 Beatrice Weasel Bear put up a peyote meeting for me so that I could have a safe trip to Scotland where I studied. She requested that I pray with the pipe in the meeting because I had done so for her father, Rex Long Visitor. In 1976 there was a thanksgiving meeting for my return and three religious traditions were brought together on the altar: the chief peyote, a document presenting a Papal Blessing from Pope Paul VI to the Native American Church on the Pine Ridge Reservation (which I obtained in Rome), and the Sacred Pipe. During the midnight water call Emerson Spider, Chief High Priest of the Church for South Dakota, talked about how remarkable the bringing together of these three religious symbols was (125–43).

6

The Sacred Pipe as an Image of Christ

I argue here that because Christian images are derived
from a common religious substratum expressed through
primal religions, behind the image of Christ is the Sacred
Pipe and its many associations. The common religious
substratum

> assumes the existence of certain irrepresentable psy-
> choid factors (33).* . . . In this "deeper" stratum we also
> find the a priori, inborn forms of "intuition," namely
> the archetypes of perception. . . . [The archetypes are]
> immediately rooted in the stuff of the organism (34–35)
> . . . [and are] the hidden foundations of the conscious
> mind . . . the roots which the psyche has sunk not only
> in the earth . . . but in the world in general. . . . They
> are inherited with the brain structure (36).

This is the religious substratum in which Christian images
have their roots. That is why primal religions, including

---

* The page numbers are cross-references within this volume.

that of the Sacred Pipe, keep one in touch with the basic religious instincts of humankind.

Identifying Christ with the Sacred Pipe is in accord with Native American tradition in which it was considered a person. The Feathered Pipe given to the Arapaho by the Thunder God was considered a brother to the Pipe Child, usually a daughter of the keeper.

As I described in the prologue, I identified Christ and the Sacred Pipe at the funeral of Rex Long Visitor when I paraphrased Scripture by saying, "I am the Living and Eternal Pipe, the Resurrection and the Life." This identification implies that the Sacred Pipe is a foreshadowing of Christ. In the words of Eliade about the cosmic tree one can ask the same basic question: Was not Christ in "some manner implied" in the Sacred Pipe and "at least vaguely felt" by the Native Americans in pre-Christian times?

There are parallels to this identification. St. Paul identified Christ with the rock that Moses struck in the desert from which water flowed (1 Cor. 10:4) And the Christian Chagga in Northern Tanzania practicing the Kikuyu religion identify Christ with the Holy Mountain, Kilimanjaro, in one of their hymns (Hallencreutz, 1979, 100).

As stated earlier, however, this identification also means that Christ needs the Sacred Pipe for His fulfillment. There is an anonymous presence of the Sacred Pipe in Christianity. Rahner writes that

> Christianity and the Church themselves have only arrived at their definitive fullness and historical maturity when the whole of salvation history and revelation his-

tory, [including the tradition of the Sacred Pipe], has visibly and explicitly been transformed into the history of Christianity and of the Church and has become a definable element in the Christianity that is explicitly embodied in the Church. . . . [They] must absorb and transform the [Sacred Pipe] into themselves in order to become fully that which they already are (58). . . . The grace of God which is intended effectively to redeem all has an incarnational character. . . . Mission and missionary actively contribute to this incarnational dynamism of grace. (62)

Consequently, Christ is incomplete without the Sacred Pipe. The tradition of the Sacred Pipe is needed to understand fully the mystery of Christ in its incarnational aspect.

The Sacred Pipe, then, is an archetypal image of wholeness. The person making a Vision Quest on top of a hill offers the pipe in the Four Directions, making himself the center of a mandala. Among the Omaha an old man lifted a small child to the Four Directions, introducing him to the cosmos, praying that all of creation would make the path of life smooth so that he would reach the four hills of life (childhood, adolescence, adulthood, and old age). This is a beautiful archetypal image of the path of individuation. And because Christ is the primary archetype of wholeness for Western man, the Sacred Pipe and its many associations are archetypal images of Christ.

According to Eliade, the Sacred Pipe "prefigures the mystery of the Incarnation. . . . The dialectic of the hierophany remains one, whether in . . . [the Sacred Pipe] or in the Incarnation of the Logos. In both cases we are faced with a manifestation, vastly different obviously, of the sacred in a fragment of the universe" (9). In addition, the Sacred Pipe represents creation because the bowl represents the earth and the stem all living things. There is, however, a presence of the cosmic Christ in creation. Eliade quotes Leon Bloy in saying that "whether the Life [of Christ] is in men, animals or plants, it is always Life, and when the moment, the imperceptible instant called death comes, it is always Christ who withdraws, as much from a tree as from a human being" (9). Rahner says that Christ is present in creation as the Word of God and as the Risen Christ. So it could be said that the Sacred Pipe as representing creation is an archetypal image of Christ.

Rahner states that if one fails to recognize the traces of God's grace in non-Christian religions, "perhaps we may only have looked too superficially and with too little love . . . [because these] religions contain quite certainly elements of a supernatural influence by grace. . . . [Christian] revelation is then the expression in objective concepts of something which [a] person has already attained" (51–52). A presence of Christ is in the Sacred Pipe because both activate the same archetype. The explicit striving toward the Sacred Pipe contained an implicit one toward Christ. The Sacred Pipe as a sacramental sign of blessing is, perhaps, the foundational reason for this presence of the anonymous Christ in the Native American psyche.

All three disciplines, depth psychology, phenomenology, and theology, give a justification for recognizing the

Sacred Pipe and its associations as archetypal images of Christ. They are the symbols through which, according to Eliade, "the immediate reality of these objects or actions 'bursts' or 'explodes' under the irruptive force of a more profound reality" (12). This more profound reality is Rahner's supernatural existential, an openness to the immediate presence of God.

Native American mythology is the basis of the identification of Christ with the Sacred Pipe. There may be a fear that Christ is being reduced to a mythological person. Although the image that becomes symbolic in the psyche and an event that becomes symbolic in history have the same archetypal value and have no psychological difference, the historical event that actuates the psyche need not be reduced to it. In Jung's words Christ is receiving the projections of the unconscious; in Eliade's, He is becoming exemplary; and, in Rahner's, there is an implicit presence of Christ.

In a Gros Ventre creation myth Earthmaker, the primeval keeper of the Flat Pipe, survived a flood by making a raft and putting the pipe on it. He sent animal survivors to the bottom to scoop up the mud from which the entire human race was born. In an Arapaho myth the pipe bowl itself is the raft. These two myths contain the same archetypal images as Noah surviving the flood in the ark. But because the ark is a symbol of the Church, the pipe bowl floating in the waters of the flood becomes the same archetypal image of Christ as does Noah's ark.

In a Hidatsa myth First Creator and Lone Man, co-makers of the earth, brought the people up from below by following a vine. Lone Man carried a wooden pipe for which First Creator ordered Male Buffalo to produce tobacco. The region below is symbolic of the unconscious, and the journey to the upper world is symbolic of the individuation process. According to Jung, Christ is the archetype of the Self, that is, of the individuation process. In psychological terms the Incarnation is equivalent to individuation. Christ can be seen as the goal of this journey made by First Creator and Lone Man.

In a Blackfoot myth a worm becomes a person holding a medicine pipe and transfers it to the man. The same symbol applies to Christ because the words of the psalmist apply to Him: "I am a worm, not a man. (Ps. 22:7)" In another one of their myths a woman married the Thunder and had two sons, and when she returned to the camp with the Medicine Pipe the Thunder had given her, he allowed her to keep their youngest son. Because of this son remaining in their midst, all the prayers offered through the pipe are answered. One can say that Christ is the Thunder Child, and because of Him one's prayers are answered.

In Wichita mythology a star named "I am a Young Man When the Dawn Comes Up" gave a black pipe and a white eagle feather to a young man at dawn. He took the pipe in a gesture of blessing and carefully blessed himself. What a beautiful archetypal image this is of Christ who is the Morning Star.

A famous Lakota myth is the woman from heaven bringing the Calf Pipe. In the Black Elk version she instructed the good hunter on how to perform seven ceremonies. This was Black Elk's attempt to bring his traditional Lakota religion and Christianity together by making the Sacred Pipe an image of Christ in the seven sacraments of the Catholic Church. Edgar Red Cloud identifies the woman with the Blessed Virgin Mary, two archetypal images of the feminine as a source of a divine mediator. In another version of the Lakota myth of the woman bringing the pipe the hunters found the woman in the middle of a buffalo herd and killed her and cut off her ears and tied them to the Calf Pipe, meaning that whatever she hears with her ears is the meaning of her generation. Christ was also killed so that He could listen to one's prayers, which allows one to understand one's life.

In the Lakota Baptiste Good winter count the woman who brings the pipe says that she is the White Buffalo Cow who spills her milk over the earth that the people may live. By milk she means the four different colored maize shown dropping from her udder. This picture is an archetypal image of nourishment but also of wholeness with the four different colored maize. It is an archetypal image of Christ nourishing and leading people to wholeness.

According to Native American tradition, the pipe stone is the blood of two rival tribes who are now reconciled because their blood is one in the pipe stone. Holding the same pipe bowl did actually achieve reconciliation as is dramatically illustrated by Densmore's account of the pipe bearer followed by four women walking back and forth, keeping peace between the angry Chippewa and Sioux warriors. The pipe stone as symbolic blood is an

archetypal image of Christ just as much as the blood of
the lamb that the Israelites sprinkled on the door post
during the exodus. As Christ is the Way and becomes the
new Exodus, so He reconciles people through His blood.
The red pipe stone is an archetypal image of the Blood of
Christ.

The pipe stone also symbolizes the blood of the original buffalo that gave the Sioux their identity, ethnically
and spiritually, as Erickson so beautifully describes:

> It is said that when the buffalo died, the Sioux died,
> ethnically and spiritually. The buffalo's body had pro-
> vided not only food and material for clothing, covering
> and shelter, but such utilities as bags and boats, strings
> for bows and for sewing, cups and spoons. Medicine
> and ornaments were made of buffalo parts; his drop-
> pings, sun dried, served as fuel in winter. Societies and
> season, ceremonies and dances, mythology and chil-
> dren's play extolled his name and image. (1945, 320)

Thus, the pipe stone as the blood of the buffalo is a beautiful archetypal image of Christ gathering the entire Sioux
way of life unto Himself. Through this image the Lakota
find their identity in Christ and the Church seeks the final
perfection of her nature, absorbing and transforming the
Lakota tradition into herself.

Among the Omaha the pipe was also the source of
identity. The pipe bearers passed by the first gens because
they were engaged in ceremonies pertaining to the taking
of life. Even to this day the other gens remind them: "You

are not people; you have no Peace Pipe." The Eucharistic presence of Christ is also the source of identity in many Christian denominations.

In a Navaho myth two boys on a journey to see their father, the Sun, were given four large pipes filled with poisonous tobacco to smoke as a test. They smoked them and remained unharmed and as a result were able to cross a rainbow bridge to their destination. Christ told the eleven apostles before His ascension that "they will pick up serpents, and if they drink any deadly thing, it will not harm them." (Mark 16:18) These are archetypal images of Christ in his power over evil.

In an Iroquois myth relating the origin of tobacco people found strange beings asleep at each end of a boat. A loud voice told them to destroy the creatures to receive a blessing. So they burned their bodies, and from the ashes rose the tobacco plant. Superhuman beings who were killed so that their flesh could become the tobacco used in ceremonies are symbolic of Christ being killed so that His flesh could be eaten in the Eucharist.

According to Menominee myth, a man stole tobacco from the gods and turned a pursuing giant into a grasshopper that became a pest to those who raise tobacco. Stealing fire and other necessities of life, which results in punishment, is a universal theme and an archetypal image of original sin.

It is, however, not only mythology but also the beliefs in the Sacred Pipe and its ceremonies that bring out archetypal images. It is not surprising that the pipe stone quarry in Minnesota was a sacred place, requiring respect and special taboos. It was the only major source of the stone used in pipes and, therefore, the source of life and all that for which the Sacred Pipe stood. Similarly, the hill of Gogatha is a sacred place that is a source of all the Eucharistic celebrations throughout the world, which makes present the one sacrifice that took place there. From this comparison one can appreciate the concept of sacred space.

Among the Arapaho the sweat lodge containing the Medicine Pipe was in the center of the camp circle so that all the tipis had this as their center. The camp became a sacred space because of the Sacred Pipe in its center. The center is an archetypal image. Among the Omaha a cedar pole representing the pipes at the center of the dance grounds is also an archetypal image of Christ. The pole was anointed, as Christ was, with a mixture of buffalo fat, the symbol of abundance, and red paint, the symbol of life, which together symbolized an abundant life. This is an archetypal image of Christ, who came that "they have life and have it more abundantly" (John 10:10).

The Arapaho blessed food with the Flat Pipe and gave the food to the people. They believed that everyone who ate the blessed food received a blessing. This is obviously an archetypal image of Holy Communion and, according to Rahner, God is working through the Arapaho's sacramental sign as well as through the Christian one. One can even say that there was an unknown presence of Christ in the ceremony. Another archetypal image of the Eucharist is the Cherokee pipe bowl with seven holes to be smoked by seven people at the same time and by passing the regular Sacred Pipe to be smoked by a circle of people.

The pipes used in Lakota societies were consecrated, set apart from profane use, by a medicine man. "He prayed over the pipe, filled it with tobacco, and sealed it with the fat from the heart of the buffalo and wrapped it in wolf skin. Now it was a medicine pipe or a sacred pipe" (148). This is an archetypal image of consecration.

A Tomahawk Pipe was used in connection with peace and war. It could be used either to kill a person or to smoke. This is an archetypal image of Christ, who said: "I have come to bring not peace but the sword. For I have come to set a man against his father, a daughter against her mother." (Matt. 34–35)

The Sacred Pipe is at the center of the Sweat Lodge Ceremony, a ceremony of purification. The need for purification was as deeply rooted among the Native Americans as among the Hebrews. Purification was undergone in order to be renewed because the sweat lodge was the womb of Mother Earth. This ceremony is certainly symbolic of both Christian asceticism and renewal.

Fasting on the hill for up to four days and nights without food or water certainly reminds one of Christ in his desert experience. If an Omaha man were under great stress, he left a filled pipe on the hill as a continuation of his prayers, a custom very similar to lighting a candle and putting it before a statue in a church. A large number of pipe bowls had animal and bird carvings on the bowls. These carvings represented the spirits through which the Native Americans prayed. They are the angels, which are related to the material world and archetypal images of the cosmic Christ present in the world of creation.

The great ceremony of the Plains tribes was the Sun Dance in which the Sacred Pipe had a very important role. This ceremony with its overwhelming sense of power is an archetypal image of sacrifice that Christ also activated by His death on the cross. This ceremony prefigured the death of Christ in a most remarkable way. George Plenty Wolf told me that when a man is pierced in the Sun Dance, he remembers the piercing of Christ.

Native Americans were concerned about preparing a person on the journey after death. The Winnebago gave not only food but a pipe and tobacco to the spirit of the deceased person to offer to the spirits it meets on the road. This external ceremony was believed to help the person spiritually and prefigures the sacraments of the anointing and viaticum (receiving Holy Communion as a preparation for death).

In the Plains Cree Masked Dance a man offered up a pipe, rotating it counterclockwise instead of clockwise as was done in every other ritual. This rotation was done by those who were called by vision to be contraries. This is an archetypal image of Christ, the Contrary, who opposed the scribes and the pharisees in their observance of the Law. It is easy not to appreciate how Christ was contrary to so much of the religious practice of the Jewish people. One can recall the long list of condemnations of the scribes and pharisee: "Woe to you scribes and pharisees (Matt. 23:13–36).

Among the Lakota "the red pipe bowl is the Indian's

blood, the blood of a woman. The stem is the breath of a man. The two together guarantee the future generations." This is an archetypal image of Christ as the source of all life.

The Sacred Pipe was used for healing. "When the Chippewa dug for medicine herbs, they offered the pipe every place they took a herb." The prayer was one of thanksgiving as well as one consecrating the herb. In a Cherokee myth a son stole tobacco from the gods. On his return "he found his father very weak, but still alive and one draw at the pipe made him strong again." During a Sioux ceremony mothers fixed the little mouths of the unconscious infants reverently on the stem of the consecrated pipe that the medicine man extended to them backward over his shoulder. The Sacred Pipe was used in many healing ceremonies and is an archetypal image of Christ the Healer.

The Mandan Buffalo Bull Dance involved a ritual use of the pipe against evil forces by pointing it at a dancer in a frightening costume who represented the evil spirit. This use of the Sacred Pipe is an archetypal image of Christ driving out the evil spirits in the Gospel story.

Two songs from the Omaha White Buffalo Hide ceremony bring out the transcendence and immanence of the Sacred Pipe. In the first song the pipe appears by its own power, apart, clothed with mysterious power. In the second song the music expresses movement toward the pipe, which now comes near and touches the supplicants. This is an archetypal image of the same transcendence and immanence found in the mystery of Christ.

Bundles containing various kinds of valuable objects were important sources of power. Special pipes are wrapped in bundles. The Calf Pipe is wrapped in a bundle at Green Grass, South Dakota. Medicine men journey there to touch their pipes to the Calf Pipe bundle so that their pipes can receive power from it. The bundle is opened on special occasions only. It is through this ceremony that the keeper receives his power. In the Keeping of the Soul Ceremony, one of the seven ceremonies associated with this pipe, a lock of hair is wrapped in a bundle and the parents take care of it for one year. The period of mourning is concluded with a pipe ceremony. An Assinboine, Comes Out Chief, wrapped the body of his six-year-old son and the pipe that he had intended to give him when he grew up in a sacred bundle. Never before had a bundle been made like that one. At night a bright light came from the bundle. The Sacred Pipe wrapped in a bundle is an archetypal image of Christ working through the sacraments.

The Menominee conducted a Tobacco Dance that reenacted the myth in which tobacco was obtained. Pete Catches on the Pine Ridge Reservation prays with his pipe in memory of his vision as the priest changes bread and wine into the body and blood of Christ in memory of the Last Supper. The ceremonial enactment of myth in primal religions gives an insight into the sacramental reenactment of Christ's life.

"Among the Winnebago the Medicine Dance Society had a ritual whose purpose was to strengthen the powers obtained in a vision." This dance had the same basic purpose as the sacrament of confirmation, which strengthens the Spirit obtained in baptism.

Many examples in the ethnographic literature show the Sacred Pipe as very sacred and to be deeply respected. The life of a Crow enemy was spared in a Lakota camp because he was in the tipi containing the Sacred Pipe. Among the Arapaho the Flat Pipe was too sacred to be transported on horseback, so only a short distance could be covered in a day's march. Strict rules had to be observed in the use of the Sacred Pipe so that severe punishment, even death, would be avoided. One had to be worthy to smoke the pipe. The Cheyenne Chief, Little Wolf, while drunk, killed Standing Elk in a fit of anger. He immediately "smashed his long-stem pipe, the symbol of the Chief's office," and he never smoked again. The reverence and respect shown the Sacred Pipe equaled that which Christians show toward the Eucharistic presence of Christ.

In a Natchez marriage ceremony the bridegroom smoked the pipe with the parents of the bride and then with his own parents. This was an expression of their commitment to each other and made it permanent. It is an archetypal image of the sacrament of matrimony.

There are many examples of the Sacred Pipe used as a means of petition. Among the Gros Ventre an old man would take his pipe, stand behind a young man, both facing the direction of the rising sun. The old man would pray that the young one would have a long life. According to a Blackfoot story, Weasel Heart parted a river that the people were unable to cross. Ever since that time they believe there was a rock shelf in the riverbed, making it easy to cross. The Native Americans smoked a pipe and left offerings of tobacco at curious places in nature as offerings to the presiding spirit of the sacred place. All these are archetypal images of Christ, the mediator who carries petitions to the Father.

During the Lakota Ghost Dance a woman remained standing near the tree throughout the dance, holding a sacred red stone pipe stretched out toward the west from which the Messiah was to appear. This woman could be taken as symbolic of the woman who brought the Sacred Pipe, whom Edgar Red Cloud identified as the Blessed Virgin Mary. Black Elk identified the Ghost Dance Messiah, who "seemed to have wounds in the palms of his hands," with Christ. The Ghost Dance Messiah is certainly an archetypal image of Christ the Messiah.

The Blackfoot appointed a man every four years to be in charge of the Sacred Pipes. To be worthy to do this he lived in a special lodge, underwent seven fasts, led a celibate life, and lived apart from his family. He was considered the "Great Medicine." This is an archetypal image of Christ the celibate.

The Sacred Pipe is frequently called the Peace Pipe because it was a primary means of establishing peace between tribes. The ceremonies in which this pipe was used had as their objective the making of sacred kinship or relatives. This ceremony took on various but related forms: the Eastern Calumet Dance, the Omaha Pipe Dance, the Sioux Making of Relatives Ceremony, and the Iroquois Eagle Dance. These ceremonies contained an implicit knowledge of Christ of whom the angels sang at His birth "peace on earth" (Luke 2:14) and Who said to the disciples on Easter Sunday evening, "Peace be with you" (John 20:19). These ceremonial dances also prefigured the Christian sacrament of baptism, whose purpose is the making of relatives because it establishes a new relationship with Christ and makes one a member of the community called the Church and is an archetypal symbol of this sacrament.

To the Osage the Sacred Pipe was the Symbolic Man. "During an address the words 'I am a person who has verily made a pipe of his body' meant symbolically that the 'pipe is the life symbol of his people'." This is a beautiful archetypal image of the Mystical Body of Christ.

Other images of the Sacred Pipe could be taken from ethnographic literature. The above images, however, are sufficient to show that the Sacred Pipe is an archetypal image of Christ.

Epilogue

It turned out to be a long journey to an understanding of the Sacred Pipe as an archetypal image of Christ that I intuited on top of the hill at Slim Butte. This understanding enlarged my vision of the spiritual quest of men and women throughout the millenniums. I came to realize that all religious traditions are expressions of the same sacred and are equal on an archetypal level. I could even claim a uniqueness for Christ without being exclusive. The understanding of my Ecumenist II position among the Oglala Laktoa matured to one of mutual fulfillment, the Sacred Pipe finding fulfillment in Christ and Christ in the Sacred Pipe. I knew now that my Christian faith was rooted in the common religious substratum of humankind, and through both the collective unconscious and the phenomenon of common religious symbols all are brought very close together. The Sacred Pipe was, indeed, an archetypal image of Christ that touched the Lakota psyche to its depths.

One arrives at a magnificent vision. In the Incarnation

Christ assumed the archetype of the Sacred Pipe as part of the psychic structure of His brain. His life can be seen as an amplification of this archetype. Christ and the Sacred Pipe are expressions of the same archetypal reality. So one may ask if the Native Americans in the past vaguely grasped Christ in the Sacred Pipe, making them open to accepting it as an explicit image of Christ today. The mythology, belief, and ceremonies of the Sacred Pipe recognized as archetypal images of Christ give a profound new understanding of Him and the Sacred Pipe. The Church must absorb this religious heritage if it is ever to achieve its full maturity.

The Readers must make their own journeys to write their own epilogues.

Appendix

Works Cited

Index

Scholarly Evaluation

The purpose of the appendix is to present the best literature for those interested in a scholarly evaluation of the three authors who were a part of my intellectual journey.

Mircea Eliade

Carl Olson interprets Eliade's scholarship "both as an attempt to understand religious phenomena and as a personal pilgrimage to the meaningful center of existence, a theme that runs throughout his works" (1992, ix). He presents brief evaluations of Eliade's critics (14–26), including Baird (1971), Dudley (1977), and Saliba (1976). Some of the criticism is the result of the tension between intuition and inductive reasoning and between phenomenological method and historical verification.

David Cave develops Eliade's contribution to a "new humanism," which addresses current issues in society (1993). He contends that despite recent critical reconsideration of Eliade's thought, which he summarizes, Eliade continues to deserve attention and has a great deal to offer on the understanding of religion. In these two works one can find answers to many of the criticisms of Eliade.

Thomas Altizer employs "Eliade as a route to a new form of theology . . . [in which] the study of non-Christian religions can be conceived of as a mode of reentry into the world of the holy . . . arriving at the meaning of the universal sacred" (1975, 13–21)). Douglas Allen states "that there are two key notions in Mircea Eliade's methodology: the dialectic of the sacred and the profane [an attempt to provide criteria to distinguish religious from other phenomena] and the central position of symbolism or symbolic structures [which provides the hermeneutical framework in terms of which Eliade interprets the meaning of religious data]" (1978, 105).

Finally, Allen and Doeing provide an extensive, although somewhat dated, annotated bibliography of Eliade's works and of secondary sources (1980).

Carl Jung

Andrew Samuels develops the nature of the archetypes and reviews the findings of ethology (the science of the study of animal behavior), biology, neurology, and structuralism. He offers an excellent critique of Jung's theory of the archetypes and the collective unconscious through a comprehensive critique of the current literature (1985, 23–54).

Anthony Stevens also develops an understanding of the archetypes, (1983). He establishes a relationship between archetypal theory and ethology. He also points out parallels between archetypal theory and the structuralist approaches in psycholinguisitcs, cognitive psychology, and anthropology. He answers difficulties concerning the division between the personal and collective unconscious. He presents a solid scientific basis of the archetypes, suggesting that the archetypes are transmitted through the DNA molecules (73) and the precise location of the archetypes in the brain structure (247–75). These are two very important books on the most recent developments on Jungian psychology.

Abundant theological interpretations of Jungian psychology have introduced readers to its problematic issues. Clifford Brown (1981, 9–36) evaluates the works of Raymond Hostie, Howard Philip, Joseph Goldbrunner, Martin Buber, Victor White, Hans Schaer, Charles Hanna, Frank Bockus, John Dunn, and Paul Tillich, all written in the 1950s and 1960s. A number of anthologies introduce readers to a large number of more contemporary critics: Robert Moore (1988), Robert Moore and Daniel Meckel (1990), Marvin Spiegelman (1988), and Murray Stein and Robert Moore (1987).

Many authors have written on Jung's relationship to Christianity, including Wallace Clift (1989) and Murray Stein (1986). Edward Edinger has a classic presentation of the place of Christ in the individuation process (1974). Morton Kelsey (1972, 1973) and John Sanford (1970, 1977) are both Episcopal priests (Sanford also is a Jungian analyst) who use whatever is good in Jungian psychology in much the same way as Thomas Aquinas used the philosophy of Aristotle.

Of special interest is John Dourley's claim that Jung located all transcendent experience within the psyche, excluding the existence of a transcendent God outside of it. Dourley uses the disagreement between Jung and theologians Martin Buber and Victor White as part of his argumentation (1995, 73–89). In response David Bock comments:

> As Jung, often said, "I am an empiricist." By this he meant
> to report only on the observable effects of experience on the

psyche. He became maddeningly opaque when challenged to declare the source of any numinous experience. Certainly, Jung was aware of the challenge that his intrapsychic model posed for traditional faith in the God who reveals himself to humanity. I believe he intended to ride the fence on this issue in his dialogue with White and Buber in the same fashion as he did in the flying saucer discussion.

Dourley summarily dismisses Jung as a contributor to a theology that claims "orthodox transcendental supernatural-ism." Is it not possible that Jung wished only to extend traditional theology into the human realm by unearthing those structures that receive the divine call by mirroring the process internally? ... It is my belief that Dr. Dourley has correctly discerned Jung's contributions to religious life, but that he has unnecessarily limited the usefulness of Jung's work to those who seek God within the psyche. I find that my own faith in a transcendent God is both enlivened and deepened by making a small adjustment in the gray area left for me by Jung's empirical position. Instead of assuming that God has arisen from the archetypes to meet my unsuspecting ego, I assume that the address of the transcendent God is spoken to the "true self" or unconscious. (1995, 92–93)

Robert C. Smith also brings out Jung's ambiguity concerning the existence of metaphysical truth outside of the psyche.

Thus on the one hand, Jung's empiricism ostensibly sought to remain within the confines of strictly scientific knowledge, which he maintained, is but one way of knowing. On the other hand, at times this same empiricism succeeded in becoming the only means of knowing (i.e., scientific reductionism). In his early writings he tried to regard psychology as an autonomous science unconcerned with any metaphysical position. In practice he was not always consistent with this theoretical position (R. Smith 1996, 114). . . . He seemingly could not decide in his own mind whether all reality is psychic or whether there is a reality that goes beyond this. He safeguarded himself by including the latter possibility. In earlier chapters we have seen how from childhood on he was of "two minds." We can now see how this double-mindedness found its way into many, if not most, of his theoretical formulations (116). . . . In Jung's later writings, he was more careful to limit himself to the psychic sphere. In *Aion* he wrote: "Psychology, as I have said, is not in a position to make metaphysical statements. It can only establish . . . the symbolism of psychic wholeness" (9ii:198). (R. Smith 1996, 117)

In his better moments Jung realized that his psychology did not give a total understanding of reality but failed to realize that other disciplines could give him a deeper understanding of his own psychology. Eliade's phenomenology and Rahner's theology allow Jung's psychology to escape its own limitations and to correct its own misunderstandings. Other disciplines do not invalidate Jung's psychology but enhance it. In doing so it becomes more meaningful to common human experience.

Finally, there is an extensive annotated bibliography on every aspect of Jungian psychology (Dyer 1991), including the relationship between religion and Jungian psychology (194–249).

Karl Rahner

Thomas Paul Sweet in his doctoral dissertation makes the assessment that "most critics feel that Rahner's work will have a profound influence on the development of theology for a long time to come, largely because of his pioneering this experiential approach, and his grounding it in a careful analysis of the emergence of transcendence" (1984, 130). William Dyck has written an excellent presentation of Rahner's thought (1992).

Kenneth D. Eberhard has an in-depth presentation of supernatural existential in his doctoral dissertation (1969). It is condensed in a journal article, which, however, does not include two critiques (1971). He considers Thomas J. Motherway as Rahner's severest critic. According to Eberhard, Motherway misunderstands Rahner's supernatural existential as a physical constituent, a thing that is added onto human nature rather than a relationship. Motherway also misunderstands Rahner's "obediential potency" as extrinsic to humans rather than intrinsic. Motherway uses the Ten Commandments as an example, saying that there is no proof that they have any effect beyond that of the moral or juridical order. Rahner, however, states that the Ten Commandments are statements about human's own reality and, therefore, an intrinsic statement about human nature. Finally, Motherway misunderstands the supernatural existential as a mediating entity (Eberhard 1969, 224–31).

> In summary we can say that if our interpretation of Rahner is correct, then all of Motherway's objections to the supernatural existential fall. When the supernatural existential is considered in terms of man's a priori horizon of God's Self-gift, then one need not look for a "thing" separate from habitual grace. Nor need one see nature as either opposed to grace or demanding it. Finally, there is no need to place man's real obligation for his personal salvation on a purely extrinsic juridical decree. (Eberhard 1969, 231)

Eberhard states that Edward Schillebeeckx is Rahner's most prominent critic. Eberhard concludes that the differences between the two theologians is nothing but a matter of semantics (Eberhard 1969, 235–41).

Eberhard has this evaluation:

> Rahner's doctrine of the supernatural existential is the clearest, most consistent, and most intelligible solution to the problem of nature and grace which we have ever encountered. It is, moreover, a microcosm of many of the major themes of Rahner's theology. By one central idea he has skillfully shown the inner affinity among the doctrines of objective redemption, divine indwelling, actual and sanctifying grace, revelation, God's universal salvific will, man's continual obligation to the supernatural, and hell's "pain of loss." Quite properly, his starting point is revelation. But the key to his whole approach lies in the philosophical method of transcendental Thomism. It is Rahner's philosophical understanding of God as man's a priori metaphysical horizon which allows him to synthesize so skillfully the nature-grace problem. (Eberhard 1971, 558)

Dom Odo Brooke has an excellent development of how the supernatural existential can be the basis for understanding natural, or non-Christian, religion (1965).

Joseph H. Wong indicates the importance of Rahner's concept of the anonymous Christian in the discussion on the relationship of the Church to non-Christian religions.

> Vatican II, with its openness and positive outlook, marked a watershed in the Church's understanding of her relationship with other religions. It has been generally acknowledged that Karl Rahner was the chief contributor to the teaching of Vatican II on this matter. The substance, if not the highly disputed term of "anonymous Christians" has been endorsed by the Council in its various documents (1994, 610).

Wong lists the most important current literature on missiology, which would introduce one to the present-day discussions (609n).

To place Rahner in the current academic discussion Wong uses three paradigms with a particular type of Christology attached to each: an "ecclesiocentric-exclusivist view with an exclusive Christology" (a position demanding an explicit knowledge of Christ and based on the axiom of no salvation outside the Church, a standard position of the Catholic Church until Vatican II); a "Christocentric-inclusivist view with a constitutive or a normative Christology," (a position that maintains the necessity and universality of Christ for salvation but demands only an implicit faith in Christ — normative, that Christ is the norm of all other revelations, constitutive, that He is the cause of salvation); and a "theocentric-plurarlist view with a non-normative Christology," (a position that maintains that salvation ultimately comes from God, who has manifested himself in different religious traditions with Jesus perceived as simply one among many mediators of salvation) (611).

Wong has an excellent treatment of Raimundo Panikkar (1981) and of Bede Griffiths (1983). He concludes with convincing arguments that Rahner, in the second paradigm, has the best solution when he presents the Holy Spirit working in all religions as the Spirit of Christ even before the Incarnation (629). Wong calls this a pneuma-Christocentrism.

Paul Knitter states that "two recent efforts, by Walbert Buhlmann and Arnulf Camps, to develop a more open theology of religions restate Rahner's basic argument" (1985, 127) Knitter, then, evaluates the objections of Hans Kung (Kung 1976, 97–99), against the position of the anonymous Christian. After careful analysis, Knitter concludes that with his understanding of Christ as normative, Kung seems to end up with much the same position that he criticized in Rahner's theory of anonymous Christianity (Knitter 1985, 131–34).

Dennis Edwards has an insightful development of the cosmic Christ that shows how Christ is related to the whole world of creation (1991).

Finally, Pedley offers an extensive unannotated bibliography of Rahner's works and secondary material arranged according to subject headings (1984).

Works Cited

Abbreviations

AP, AMNH	Anthropological Papers, American Museum of Natural History. New York, N.Y.
AR, BAE	Annual Report, Bureau of American Ethnology. Washington, D.C.
B, AMNH	Bulletin, American Museum of Natural History. New York N.Y.
B, BAE	Bulletin, Bureau of American Ethnology. Washington, D.C.
JAFL	Journal of American Folklore.
NAB	New American Bible

Alexander, Hartly Burr. 1967. *The World's Rim: Great Mysteries of the North American Indian.* Lincoln: Univ. of Nebraska Press.

Allen, Douglas. 1978. *Structure and Creativity in Religion: Hermeneutics in Mircea Eliade's Phenomenology and New Directions.* The Hague: Mouton.

Allen, Douglas, and Dennis Doeing. 1980. *Mircea Eliade: An Annotated Bibliography.* New York: Garland.

Altizer, Thomas J. J. 1975. *Mircea Eliade and the Dialectic of the Sacred.* Philadelphia: Westminster Press.

Baird, Robert D. 1971. *Category Formation and the History of Religions.* The Hague: Mouton.

Ball, Sydney H. 1941. "The Mining of Gems and Ornamental Stones by American Indians." *B,BAE* 128:1–77.

Barrett, S. A. 1911. "The Dream Dance of the Chippewa and Menomini Indians of Northern Wisconsin." *Bulletin of the Milwaukee Public Museum* 1: 251–406.

Beckwith, M. W. 1930. "Mythology of the Oglala Dakota." *JAFL* 43:339–406.

Beirnaert, S. J., Louis. 1949. "La dimension mythique dans le sacramentalisme chrétien." *Eranos-Jahrbuch* 17:255–286.

———. 1951. "The Mythic Dimension in Christian Sacramentalism." *Cross Currents* 2:68–86. (This English translation of Beirnaert differs slightly from that found in Eliade 1991.)

Bock, David C. 1995. "A Reply to John P. Dourley." *International Journal for the Psychology of Religion* 5:91–94.

Bockus, Frank. 1968. "The Archetypal Self: Theological Values in Jung's Psychology." In *The Dialogue Between Theology and Psychology,* edited by Peter Homans, 221–47. Chicago: Univ. of Chicago Press.

Bowers, Alfred W. 1965. "Hidatsa Social and Ceremonial Organization." *B, BAE* 194.

Brooke, Dom Odo. 1965. "Natural Religion in the Supernatural Existential." In *The Downside Review* (272) 84:201–12.

Brown, Clifford A. 1981. *Jung's Hermeneutic of Doctrine: Its Theological Significance.* Ann Arbor, Mich.: Scholars Press.

Brown, Joseph Epes. 1953. *The Sacred Pipe: Black Elk's Account of the Seven Rites of the Oglala Sioux.* Norman: Univ. of Oklahoma Press.

Buhlmann, Walbert. 1983. *God's Chosen Peoples.* Maryknoll, N.Y.: Orbis Books.

Camps, Arnold. 1983. *Partners in Dialogue: Christianity and Other World Religions.* Maryknoll, N.Y.: Orbis Books.

Carter, John C. 1938. "The Northern Arapaho Flat Pipe and the Ceremony of Covering the Pipe." *B,BAE* 119:69–102.

Catlin, George. 1841. *Letters and Notes on Manners, Customs and Conditions of the North American Indian.* 2 vols. London: The Author.

————. 1967. *O-Kee-Pa: A Religious Ceremony and Other Customs of the Mandans.* New Haven, Conn.: Yale Univ. Press.

————. 1979. *Indian Art in Pipestone: George Catlin's Portfolio in the British Museum,* edited by John C. Ewers. Washington, D.C.: Smithsonian Institution.

Cave, David. 1993. *Mircea Eliade's Vision for a New Humanism.* New York: Oxford Univ. Press.

Chittenden, H. M., and A. T. Richardson, eds. 1905. *Life, Letters and Travels of Fr. Pierre Jean DeSmet, S. J. 1801–1873.* 4 vols. New York: Harper.

Clift, Wallace B. 1989. *Jung and Christianity: The Challenge of Reconciliation.* New York: Crossroad.

Collins, Dabney Otis. 1969. "A Happening at Oglala." *American West* 6:15–19.

Cooper, John M. 1940. "The Religion of the Gros Ventres of Montana." *Annals Lateranense* (Rome) 4:97–115.

————. 1957. *Gros Ventres of Montana.* Pt. 2, *Religion.* Anthropological Series no. 16. Washington, D.C.: Catholic Univ. of America.

Curtin, Jeremiah, and I. N. Howitt. 1910–11. "Seneca Fiction. Legends and Myths." *AR, BAE* 32:37–813.

Curtis, Edward. 1907–30. *North American Indians of the United States and Alaska*. Vols. 1, 4, 6, and 19 of 20 vols. Cambridge, Mass.: Univ. Press.

Deloria, Ella. 1929. "The Sun Dance of the Oglala Sioux." *JAFL* 42:354–413.

———. 1938. *Teton Sioux Folklore and Ethnology*. Ms. 259, Bushotter Texts, Library of the American Philosophical Society. Philadelphia.

DeMallie, Raymond J., ed. 1984. *The Sixth Grandfather: Black Elk's Teaching Given to John G. Neihardt*. Lincoln: Univ. of Nebraska Press.

Denig, Edwin T. 1928–29. "Indian Tribes of the Upper Missouri." *AR, BAE* 46:375–628.

Densmore, Frances. 1913. "Chippewa Music." *B, BAE* 13.

———. 1918. "Teton Sioux Music." *B, BAE* 61.

———. 1929. 'Chippewa Customs.' *B, BAE* 86.

Dixon, Roland. 1899. "Color Symbolism of the Cardinal Points." *JAFL* 12:10–16.

Dodge, R. I. 1877. *The Plains of the Great West and Their Inhabitants*. New York: C. P. Putnam's Sons.

Domenech, Emmanuel. 1860. *Seven Years Residence in the Great Deserts of North America*. 2 vols. London.

Dorsey, George. 1906. "Legend of the Teton Medicine Pipe." *JAFL* 19:326–29.

Dorsey, James. 1881–82. "Omaha Sociology." *AR, BAE* 3:205–370.

———. 1889–90. "A Study of Siouan Cults." *AR, BAE* 11:351–544.

———. 1893–94. "Siouan Sociology: A Posthumous Paper." *AR, BAE* 15: 205–44.

Dourley, John P. 1995. "The Religious Significance of Jung's

Psychology." In *International Journal for the Psychology of Religion* 5:73–89.

Dudley III, Guilford. 1977. *Religion on Trial: Mircea and His Critics.* Philadelphia: Temple Univ. Press.

Dusenberry, Verne. 1962. "Montana Cree: A Study in Religious Persistence." *Stockholm Studies in Comparative Religion* 3.

Dyck, S.J., William V. 1992. *Karl Rahner.* Collegeville, Minn.: Liturgical Press.

Dyer, Donald R. 1991. *Cross-Currents of Jungian Thought: An Annotated Bibliography.* Boston: Shambhala.

Eberhard, Kenneth D. 1969. "Karl Rahner's Doctrine of the Supernatural Existential." Ph.D diss., Graduate Theological Union, Berkeley, Calif.

———. 1971. "Karl Rahner and the Supernatural Existential." *Thought* (183) 65:537–61.

Edinger, Edward F. 1974. *Ego and Archetype: Individuation and the Religious Function of the Psyche.* Baltimore, Md.: Penguin Books.

Edwards, Dennis. 1991. *Jesus and the Cosmos.* New York: Paulist Press.

Eliade, Mircea. 1958. *Patterns in Comparative Religion.* New York: Sheed and Ward.

———. 1959. "Methodological Remarks on the Study of Religious Symbolism." In *The History of Religions: Essays in Methodology,* edited by Mircea Eliade and Joseph M. Kitagawa, 86–107. Chicago: Univ. of Chicago Press.

———. 1961. *The Sacred and the Profane: The Nature of Religion.* New York: Harper and Row.

———. 1991. *Images and Symbols: Studies in Religious Symbolism.* Princeton, N.J.: Princeton Univ. Press.

Erikson, Erik. 1945. "Childhood and Tradition in Two American Indian Tribes." In *The Psychoanalytic Study of the Child* 1:319–50.

Ewers, John C. 1963. "Blackfoot Indian Pipes and Pipe Making." *B, BAE* 186: 29–60.

———. 1986. *Plains Indian Sculpture: A Traditional Art from America's Heartland*. Washington, D.C.: Smithsonian Institution Press.

Fenton, William N. 1953. "The Iroquois Eagle Dance, An Offshoot of the Calumet Dance." *B, BAE* 156.

Fewkes, J. Walter. 1895–96. "Archaeological Expedition to Arizona in 1895." *AR, BAE* 17:519–744.

Fletcher, Alice. 1884. "White Buffalo Festival of the Uncpapa; Elk Mystery or Festival; Religious Ceremony of the Four Winds or Quarters as Observed by the Santee Sioux; The 'Wawan' or Pipe Dance of the Omaha." *Report Peabody Museum of American Archaeology and Ethnology* 16, no. 3:260–333.

———. 1892. *"Hae' Thu-Sha* Society of the Omaha Tribe." *JAFL* 5:135–44.

———. 1900–1901. "The Hako: A Pawnee Ceremony." *AR, BAE* 22, pt. 2.

Fletcher, Alice, and Francis LaFlesche. 1905–6. "The Omaha Tribe." *AR, BAE* 27. Reprinted as *The Omaha Tribe*. 2 vols. Lincoln: Univ. of Nebraska, 1972.

Fowke, Gerald. 1891–92. "Stone Art." *AR, BAE* 13:47–178.

Goddard, Pliny Earle. 1914. "Dancing Societies of the Sarsi Indians." *AP, AMNH* 11:461–74. (The entire eleventh volume on the societies of the Plains Indians contains references to the pipe.)

———. 1918. "Myths and Tales of the San Carlos Apache." *AP, AMNH* 24:1–86.

Griffiths, Bede. 1983. *The Cosmic Revelation: The Hindu Way to God.* Springfield, Ill.: Templegate.

Grinnell, George. 1972. *The Cheyenne Indians: Their History and Ways of Life.* 2 vols. New Haven, Conn.: Yale Univ. Press.

Hallencreutz, Carl F. 1979. "Christ Is the Mountain: Some Observations on the Religious Functions of Symbols in the Encounter of Christianity and Other Religions." In *Religious Symbols and Their Functions,* edited by Harald Biezais. Stockholm: Almqvist and Wiksell.

Harrington, John P. 1932. "Tobacco among the Karuk Indians of California." *B, BAE* 94.

Hassrick, Royal B. 1964. *The Sioux: Life and Customs of a Warrior Society.* Norman: Univ. of Oklahoma Press.

Healy, Kathleen. 1990. *Christ as Common Ground: A Study of Christianity and Hinduism.* Pittsburgh: Duquesne Univ. Press.

Henshaw, Henry W. 1880–1881. "Animal Carvings from the Mounds of the Mississippi Valley." *AR, BAE* 2: 117–66.

Hilger, Sr. M. Inez. 1951. "Chippewa Child Life and Its Cultural Background." *B, BAE* 146.

———. 1952. "Arapaho Child Life and Its Cultural Background." *B, BAE* 148.

Hodge, Frederick Webb, ed. 1910. "Handbook of American Indians North of Mexico." 2 vols. *B, BAE* 30.

Hoffman, W. J. 1885–86. "The Mide'wiwin or 'Grand Medicine' Society of the Ojibwa." *AR, BAE* 7:143–300.

———. 1892–93. "The Menomini Indians." *AR, BAE* 14:3–328.

Holler, Clyde. 1995. *Black Elk's Religion: The Sun Dance and Lakota Catholicism.* Syracuse, N.Y.: Syracuse Univ. Press.

Holmes, W. H. 1919. "Handbook of Aboriginal Antiquities." *B, BAE* 60.

Howard, James. 1965. "The Ponca Tribe." *B, BAE* 195.

Hultkrantz, Åke. 1969. "Religious Syncretism among the Shoshoni." In *Syncretism,* edited by Sven S. Hartmen, 15–40. Stockholm: Scripta Instituti Donneriani Aboensis III.

Jones, J. A. 1955. "The Sun Dance of the Northern Ute." *B, BAE* 157:203–63.

Jung, Carl. 1953–86. *Collected Works.* Vols. 4, 5, 7, 8, 9i, 10, 11, 12, and 18. Princeton, N.J.: Princeton Univ. Press.

Kelsey, Morton. 1972. *Encounter with God: A Theology of Christian Experience.* New York: Paulist Press.

———. 1973. *Healing and Christianity.* New York: Harper and Row.

Kemnitzer, Luis. 1970. "The Cultural Provenience of Objects Used in Yuwipi: A Modern Teton Dakota Healing Ritual." *Ethnos* 35:40–75.

Kennedy, Michael, ed. 1961. *The Assineboines: From the Accounts of the Old Ones Told to First Boy.* Norman: Univ. of Oklahoma Press.

Knitter, Paul F. 1985. *No Other Name? A Critical Survey of Christian Attitudes Toward the World Religions.* Maryknoll, N.Y.: Orbis Books.

Kroeber, Alfred. 1902–7. "The Arapaho. III. Ceremonial Organization." *B, AMNH* 18

———. 1907. "Gros Ventre Myths and tales." *AP, AMNH.*1:55–139.

———. 1908. "Ethnology of the Gros Ventre." *AP, AMNH.*1:141–281.

———. 1925. "Handbook of the Indians of California." *B, BAE* 78.

Kung, Hans. 1976. *On Being a Christian.* Garden City, N.Y.: Doubleday.

LaFlesche, Francis. 1914–15. "The Osage Tribe: Rite of the Chiefs; Sayings of the Ancient One." *AR, BAE*36.

———. 1917–18. "The Osage Tribe: The Rite of Vigil." *AR, BAE* 39.

———. 1927–28. "The Osage Tribe: Rite of Wa-xo-be." *AR, BAE* 45.

———. 1939. "War Ceremony and Peace Ceremony of the Osage Indians." *B, BAE* 101.

Llewellyn, K. N., and E. Adamson Hoebel. 1941. *The Cheyenne Way: Conflict and Case Law in Primitive Jurisprudence.* Norman: Univ. of Oklahoma Press.

Looking Horse, Stanley. 1977. Personal conversation with the author. October. Green Grass, S.D.

Lowie, Robert H. 1909. "The Assinboine." *AP, AMNH*4:1–270.

———. 1913. "Societies of the Crow, Hidatsa and Mandan Indians." *AP, AMNH* 11:143–358.

———. 1920. "The Tobacco Society of the Crow Indians." *AP, AMNH* 21:101–200.

Lynn, James W. 1889. "The Religion of the Dakotas." *Collection of the Minnesota Historical Society* 2:142–74.

McGee, W. J. 1893–94. "The Siouan Indians: A Preliminary Sketch." *AR, BAE* 15:153–204.

McGuire, Joseph D. 1899. *Pipe and Smoking Customs of the American Aborigines, Based on Material in the U.S. National Museum.* Report of the U.S. National Museum, Washington, D.C.

Mallery, Garrick. 1888–89. "Picture-writing of the American Indians." *AR, BAE* 10.

Mandelbaum, David. G. 1940. "The Plains Cree." *AP, AMNH* 37:155–316.

Mayhall, Mildred. 1962. *The Kiowas.* Norman: Univ. of Oklahoma Press.

Meekel, Scudder. n.d. "Field Notes on Lakota Indians." Typed manuscript in authors's possession.

Michaelson, Truman. 1921. "The Owl Sacred Pack of the Fox Indians." *B, BAE* 72.

Miller, David Leroy. 1981. *Christs: Meditation on Archetypal Images of Christian Theology.* New York: Seabury Press.

———. 1995. "Biblical Imagery and Psychological Likeness." In *Jung and the Interpretation of the Bible,* edited by David L. Miller, 102–12. New York: Continuum.

Mooney, James. 1892–93. "The Ghost-Dance Religion and the Sioux Outbreak of 1890." *AR, BAE* 14:641–1110.

———. 1895–96. "Calendar History of the Kiowa Indians." *AR, BAE* 17:129–445.

———. 1897–98. "Myths of the Cherokee." *AR, BAE* 19.

Moore, Robert L., ed. 1988. *Carl Jung and Christian Spirituality.* New York: Paulist Press.

Moore, Robert L., and Daniel J. Meckel, eds. 1990. *Jung and Christianity in Dialogue: Faith, Feminism, and Hermeneutics.* New York: Paulist Press.

Motherway, Thomas J. 1965. "Supernatural Existential." *Chicago Studies* 4:79–103.

Murdoch, John. 1887–88. "Ethnological Results of the Point Barrow Expedition." *AR, BAE* 9.

Murie, James R. 1914. "Pawnee Indian Societies." *AP, AMNH* 11:542–644.

Neihardt, John. 1961. *Black Elk Speaks: Being the Life Story of a Holy Man of the Oglala Sioux.* Lincoln: Univ. of Nebraska Press.

Nicollet, L. N. 1843. Nicollet "Report Intended to Illustrate Map of the Hydrographic Basin of the Upper Mississippi River." 26th Cong., 2d sess., S. Doc. W7.

Nomland, Gladys A. 1931. "A Bear River Shaman's Curative Dance." *American Anthropologist* 33:38–41.

Olson, Carl. 1992. *The Theology and Philosophy of Eliade: A Search for the Centre*. New York: St. Martin's Press.

Panikkar, Raimundo. 1981. *The Unknown Christ of Hinduism: Towards an Ecumenical Christophany*. Rev. ed. Maryknoll, N.Y.: Orbis Books.

Paper, Jordan. 1988. *Offering Smoke: The Sacred Pipe and Native American Religion*. Moscow: Univ. of Idaho.

Pedley, S.J., C. J. 1984. "An English Bibliographical Aid to Karl Rahner." *Heythrop Journal* 25:319–65.

Pepper, George, and Gilbert L. Wilson. 1907. "An Hidatsa Shrine and the Beliefs Respecting It." *Memoirs of the American Anthropological Association* 2: 1275–328.

Pond, Gidean H. 1860–67. "Dakota Superstitions." *Collection of the Minnesota Historical Society* 1:215–25.

Powell, Peter J. 1969. *Sweet Medicine: The Continuing Role of the Sacred Arrows, the Sun Dance and the Sacred Buffalo Hat in Northern Cheyenne History*.2 vols. Norman: Univ. of Oklahoma Press.

Powers, William K. 1987. *Beyond the Vision: Essays on American Indian Culture*. Norman: Univ. of Oklahoma Press.

Radin, Paul. 1911. "The Ritual and Significance of the Winnebago Medicine Dance." *JAFL* 24:149–208.

———. 1915–16. "The Winnebago tribe." *AR, BAE* 17. Reprinted as *The Winnebago Tribe*. 1970. Lincoln; Univ. of Nebraska Press.

Rahner, Karl. 1961–91. *Theological Investigations*. Vols. 1, 4, 5, 6, 10, 11, 12, 14, and 18. New York: Seabury Press.

———. 1969. "Resurrection. D Theology." In *Sacramentum Mundi: An Encyclopedia of Theology*, edited by Karl Rahner et al., 331–33. New York: Herder and Herder.

Reichard, Gladys. 1970. *Navajo Religion: A Study of Symbolism.* Princeton, N.J.: Princeton Univ. Press.

Reigert, W. A. 1975. *Quest for the Pipe of the Sioux.* Rapid City, S.D.: Privately printed.

Ricketts, Mac Linscott. 1970. "The Nature and Extent of Eliade's 'Jungianism'." *Union Seminary Quarterly Review* 25:211–34.

Riggs, Stephen R. 1869. *Tah-koo Wahkan: The Gospel among the Dakota.* Boston: Congregational Sabbath School.

Roberts, Jr., Frank H. 1931. "The Ruins at Kiatuthlanna, Eastern Arizona." *B, BAE* 100.

Ross, Alexander. 1956. *The Fur Hunters of the Far West.* Norman: Univ. of Oklahoma Press.

Saliba, John. 1976. *'Homo Religiosus' in Mircea Eliade: An Anthropological Evaluation.* Leiden: E. J. Brill.

Samuels, Andrew. 1985. *Jung and the Post-Jungians.* Boston: Routledge and Kegan Paul.

Sanford, John A. 1970. *The Kingdom Within.* New York: J. B. Lippincott.

———. 1977. *Healing and Wholeness.* New York: Paulist Press.

Schillebeeckx, Edward. 1964. "L'instinct de la foi selon S. Thomas d' Aquin." *Revue des sciences philosophiques et theologiques* 48:377–408.

Schoolcraft, Henry. 1856. *Information Reflecting the History, Condition and Prospects of the Indian Tribes of the U.S.* 6 vols. Philadelphia: Lippincott.

Shimkin, D. B. 1953. "The Wind River Shoshone Sun Dance." *B,BAE* 151:397–484.

Simms, S. C. 1904. "Cultivation of 'Medicine Tobacco. by the Crows: A Preliminary Paper." *American Anthropologist* 6:331–35.

Skinner, Alanson. 1914. "Political Organization, Cults and Ceremonies of the Plains-Ojibwa and Plains Cree Indians." *AP, AMNH* 11:475–542.

———. 1915. "Associations and Ceremonies of the Menomini Indians." *AP, AMNH* 13:167–215.

Smith, Erminnie. 1880–81. "Myths of the Iroquois." *AR, BAE* 2:47–116.

Smith, John F. 1964. "A Ceremony for the Preparation of the Offering Cloths for Presentation to the Sacred Calf Pipe." *Plains Anthropologist* 9:190–96.

———. 1967. "A Short History of the Sacred Calf Pipe." *University of South Dakota Museum News* 28:1–37.

Smith, Robert C. 1996. *The Wounded Jung: Effects of Jung's Relationships on His Life and Work.* Evanston, Ill.: Northwestern Univ. Press.

Spiegelman, J. Marvin, ed. 1988. *Catholicism and Jungian Psychology.* Phoenix, Ariz.: Falcon Press.

Spier, Leslie. 1921. "The Sun Dance of the Plains Indians: Its Development and Diffusion." *AP, AMNH* 16: 451–527. (The entire sixteenth volume on the Sun Dances of Plains Indians contains references to the pipe.)

Squier, E. G., and E. H. Davis. 1848. "Ancient Monuments of the Mississippi Valley Comprising the Results of Extensive Original Surveys and Explorations." Washington D.C.: *Smithsonian Contributions to Knowledge* 1.

Stands in Timber, John, and Margot Liberty. 1967. *Cheyenne Memories.* New Haven, Conn.: Yale Univ. Press.

Stein, Murray. 1986. *Jung's Treatment of Christianity: The Psychotherapy of a Religious Tradition.* Wilmette, Ill: Chiron.

Stein, Murray, and Robert L. Moore, eds. 1987. *Jung's Challenge to Contemporary Religion.* Wilmette, Ill.: Chiron.

Steinmetz, S. J., Paul B. 1984. "The Sacred Pipe in American Indian Religions." *American Indian Culture and Research Journal* 8:27–80.

———. 1990. *Pipe, Bible and Peyote among the Oglala Lakota: A Study in Religious Identity.* Knoxville: Univ. of Tennessee Press.

Stevens, Anthony. 1983. *Archetypes: A Natural History of the Self.* New York: Quill.

Stolzman, S.J., William. 1986. *The Pipe and Christ: A Christian-Sioux Dialogue.* Chamberlain, S.D.: St. Joseph Indian School.

Swanton, John R. 1924–25. "Social Organization and Social Usages of the Indians of the Creek Confederacy." *AR, BAE* 42:23–472.

———. 1946. "The Indians of the Southeastern United States." *B, BAE* 137.

Sweet, Thomas Paul. 1984. "Transcending: Its Accessibility and Theological Significance." Ph.D. diss., Graduate Theological Union, Berkeley, Calif.

Teit, James A. 1927–28. "The Saleshan Tribes of the Western Plateau." *AR, BAE* 45:23–396.

Thomas, Sidney. 1941. "A Sioux Medicine Bundle." *American Anthropologist* 43:605–9.

Thwaites, Reuben, ed. 1896–1901. *The Jesuit Relations and Allied Documents: Travels and Explorations of the Jesuit Missionaries in New France.* Cleveland, Ohio: Burroughs Brothers. Reprinted as *Jesuit Relations and Allied Documents: The American West.* 73 vols. in 36. Chicago: Loyola Univ. Press, 1959.

———. 1904–7. *Early Western Travelers, 1748–1846.* Vols. 2, 5, 13, 23, 24, 27, and 28 of 32 vols. Cleveland: Arthur Clarke.

Voget, Fred W. 1953. "Current Trends in the Wind River Shoshone Sun Dance." *B, BAE* 151:485–99.

Walker, James R. 1917. "The Sun Dance and Other Ceremonies of the Oglala Division of the Teton Dakota." *AP, AMNH* 16:51–221.

———. 1980. *Lakota Belief and Ritual,* edited by Raymond J. DeMallie and Elaine A. Jahner. Lincoln: Univ. of Nebraska Press.

———. 1982. *Lakota Society,* edited by Raymond J. DeMallie. Lincoln: Univ. of Nebraska.

Wallace, Ernest, and E. Adamson Hoebel. 1952. *The Comanche: Lords of the South Plains.* Norman: Univ. of Oklahoma Press.

Wallis, W. E. 1923. "Beliefs and Tales of the Canadian Dakota." *JAFL* 36:36–104.

Warren, William W. 1885. "History of the Ojibway Based upon Traditions and Oral Statements." *Collection of the Minnesota Historical Society* 5:21–394.

Waters, Frank. 1963. *Book of the Hopi.* New York: Viking.

Wedel, W. R. 1961. *Prehistoric Man on the Great Plains.* Norman: Univ. of Oklahoma Press.

West, George A. 1934. Tobacco. "Pipes and Smoking Customs of the American Indian." *Bulletin of the Public Museum of Milwaukee* 17, 2 pts. (Pt. 1 is text, and pt. 2 is a complete set of photographs.)

Wissler, Clark. 1908. "Mythology of the Blackfoot Indian." *AP, AMNH* 2:1–163.

———. 1912. "Societies and Ceremonial Associations in the Oglala Division of the Teton Dakota." *AP, AMNH* 11:1–99.

———. 1913. "Societies and Dance Associations of the Blackfoot Indians." *AP, AMNH* 11:359–460.

———. 1966. *Indians of the United States.* New York: Doubleday.

Wong, Joseph H. 1994. "Anonymous Christians: Karl Rahner's Pneuma-Christocentrism and an East-West Dialogue." *Theological Studies* 55:609–37.

Index

Angels 67–68

Anonymous Christian, 51–53, 59–60; and archetypal psychology, 82

Archetypes: and biological inheritance, 30–31; as bridges between matter and spirit, 35–36; and evolution, 32; as foundation of Christian experience, 46–48; and human experience, 36–37; and instincts, 34–35; and numinosity, 37; rediscovery through Christianity of, 24–25; and relationship between Christ and non-Christian religions, 83–86; of the self, 41–42

Beirnaert, Louis, 19–21

Buffalo Calf Pipe: and Nicholas Black Elk, 110–11; and Finger, 112; and Iron Shell, 114; and J. M. Lee, 114; and Lone Man, 113–14; and Garrick Mallery, 114; and Percy Phillips, 113; and John Smith, 113; and George Sword, 112; and Ernest Two Runs, 113; and Thomas Tyon, 112

Calumet: diffusion of, 150; meaning of, 150–52; use of, 152–56

Christ: as an archetypal image, 40–41; as archetypal and as historical, 83–86; as the end of creation, 86–87; and the